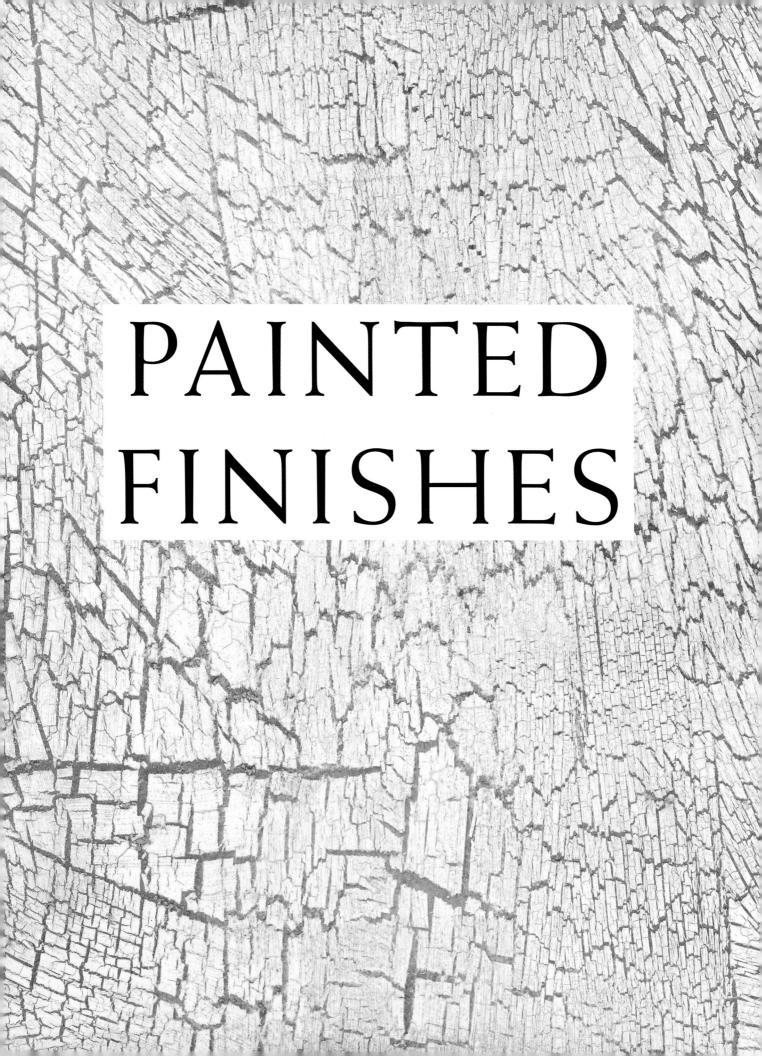

# PAINTED

# FINISHES

# PAINTED
# FINISHES
## for Walls & Furniture

Easy Techniques
for Great
New Looks

BY
SUSAN GOANS DRIGGERS

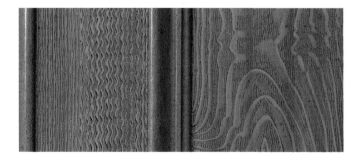

Sterling Publishing Co., Inc. New York

## Prolific Impressions Production Staff:

Editor: Mickey Baskett
Photography: Jeff Herr, Jerry Mucklow
Copy: Phyllis Mueller
Graphics: Dianne Miller, Michael Moore
Styling: Laney McClure
Proofing: Jim Baskett

## Susan Goans Driggers wishes to thank the following:

Mickey & Jim Baskett
Donna & Gordon Brady
Mary Clark
Susan Fowlkes
Mary Gilmore
Ira Franklin Goans
Suzette Faith Goans
Byron Holmes
Cathy Kicklighter
Linda Middleton

Beverly & David Montgomery
Linda & Norman Nash
Gary Palmer
Larry & Beth Rymer
Linda & Jerry Titus
Charles Wood
Ruth & David Wray
Plaid Enterprises Inc., Norcross, Ga, for supplying paint and finishing products.

Library of Congress Cataloging-in-Publication Data Available

1   3   5   7   9   10   8   6   4   2

First paperback edition published in 1999 by
Sterling Publishing Company, Inc.
387 Park Avenue South, New York, N.Y. 10016
© 1998 by Prolific Impressions, Inc.
Distributed in Canada by Sterling Publishing
℅ Canadian Manda Group, One Atlantic Avenue, Suite 105
Toronto, Ontario, Canada M6K 3E7
Distributed in Great Britain and Europe by Cassell PLC
Wellington House, 125 Strand, London WC2R 0BB, England
Distributed in Australia by Capricorn Link (Australia) Pty Ltd.
P.O. Box 6651, Baulkham Hills, Business Centre, NSW 2153, Australia

*Printed in Hong Kong*
*All rights reserved*
Sterling ISBN 0-8069-9441-X Trade
0-8069-9416-9 Paper

# CONTENTS

# INTRODUCTION

Decorating our homes and making them personal has become a pleasurable pastime for many. Transforming the "not-so-pretty" into something gorgeous is surprisingly simple and lots of fun, and can result in a great source of pride. This book will introduce you to many exciting techniques that are not only easy to achieve but fun and beautiful as well.

Using ordinary latex paints and easy to find tools and supplies, this book shows how to create a variety of textured finishes and faux finishes for walls and furniture. The techniques will show how to create the look of stone, wood graining, wood inlay, marble, plus ragged, sponged, and brush textured finishes. The appearance of age and wear can be added almost instantly with crackling, aged plaster, antiquing, distressing, and spattering. And you will learn how simple techniques such as stenciling, stamping, and design painting can be used to give walls and furniture a professional look.

The room and furniture projects presented here—more than 30 in all—are suitable for a wide range of decorating styles. Photographs show entire room treatments, supplies and tools needed, technique how-to photos and step-by-step details of work in progress. When needed, design patterns are included for cutting your own stencils and painted designs.

So roll up your sleeves and make your house your own by creating one-of-a-kind interiors.

# A Word From the Artist

One afternoon while sponging a wall in a historic house in Olglethorpe County, Georgia, I found myself peering out the window. The wood in the house, probably from trees that once grew on the site, had been hand hewn in 1820 by a master craftsman who obviously had taken great pride in his labor. I wondered if the craftsman had stopped working as I did now, pausing for a brief moment to view the rich green foliage outside the window.

The gorgeous natural scene outside the window caught my eye as I felt the gentle breeze of the sultry Southern afternoon. The birds serenaded me with their songs, and the church bell chimes seemed to float through the air. Truly this was a day the Lord had made just for me to enjoy as I worked. I was so taken with my surroundings and was so enjoying my work that the long hours of labor seemed moments, as if I were adding only a few strokes of color to this already beautiful setting. The quietness of the land seemed to hold me in a restful state. I thought, "How great my God is to allow me to add my talent to this room and even greater, to be able to share it with others through the pages of this book."

As I worked on various rooms for this book, the hours of labor had been long, but each project was chosen with much thought so that each page, whether simple or elegant, would be filled with beauty. I wish I could share all the pleasures I found while working on the projects for this book—the homes that had been opened up to me with such gracious hospitality and love was a real source of joy. Everyone involved shared their talents and invested time and effort to help me inspire you to create your own labor of love in your home.

SUSAN GOANS DRIGGERS

# PAINT PRODUCTS

*The paint products used to create the finishes in this book are readily available and inexpensive. All paint products used are latex (or acrylic) based products.* **Caution: do not attempt to mix a latex-based product with an oil-based product.** *Look for the paint products used here at paint stores, the paint departments of hardware and home improvement centers, and at crafts stores.*

## • LATEX WALL PAINT

Latex wall paint can be used to create almost every technique in this book. Choose an eggshell or satin sheen (rather than flat or gloss). It is used to paint walls and furniture and can be mixed with a clear glazing medium to create ragged, sponged, and brushed textures and faux finishes such as marbleizing and faux stone. Latex paint is available in a huge array of colors and can be custom mixed, so the color selection is limitless. Follow the manufacturer's instructions for application and drying and curing times.

## • ACRYLIC CRAFT PAINT

Acrylic craft paint is used for decorative design painting and can also be used for stenciling and stamping. Also, it is an ideal substitute for latex paint when a small amount is all you need (if you're basecoating a small area, for example, or adding color to a small amount of glazing medium). It comes in plastic squeeze bottles in a variety of colors.

## • COLORED PAINT GLAZES AND STENCIL GEL PAINTS

Colored paint glazes (acrylic) and stencil gel paints (acrylic) are transparent paints with a gel-like consistency. They can be used to tint clear glazing medium for sponging, ragging, and mopping walls. The paint, directly from the bottle can be used for stenciling and stamping.

## • GLAZING MEDIUM

Glazing medium is a colorless, full-bodied liquid or gel acrylic that gets its color by tinting it with latex paint, acrylic craft paint, or gel paint. After coloring the neutral glaze, it is used for ragging, sponging, color washing, brushed textures, and a variety of faux finishes. When paint is mixed into the neutral glazing medium, the pigmentation of the paint is thinned, creating a translucent color.

## • PRIMERS

Primers are applied to surfaces to block stains and seal the surface after the surface has been prepared for painting but before the basecoat is applied. Primers are available in spray or brush-on form and contain a white pigment. DO NOT use a primer if you plan to color wash or stain the surface or if the faux finish you are applying involves distressing after painting. (The white primer would show through, ruining the effect.)

## • STAINS

Premixed stains are transparent layers of color that, when applied to wood, allow the wood's grain and character to show through. They are available as liquids and in pump spray bottles. You can also make your own wood stains by mixing glazing medium with latex paint, acrylic craft paint, or colored paint glaze. See the "Color Washing" section of this book for instructions.

## • CRACKLE MEDIUM

Crackle medium is a clear, easy to apply liquid. Crackle medium does not crack, but any water-based medium that is applied on top of the dried medium reacts with it by shrinking and cracking, creating the distinctive crackled look. This product is available in most craft shops or do-it-yourself stores.

## • VARNISHES

Clear varnish is a brush-on water base finish that is used to seal surfaces and as the topcoat in the one-color crackle process. Choose a varnish that is appropriate for the paint you're using. Follow the manufacturer's instructions for application and drying time.

## • SEALERS

Sealers are used for sealing raw wood or as a protective topcoat after painting, staining, or glazing. Sealers come in liquid and spray form. Choose a sealer that's non-yellowing, quick-drying, and appropriate for the paint you're using. Follow the manufacturer's instructions for application and drying time. Several thin coats are better than one thick coat.

For sealing raw wood, use a matte sealer. When using as a topcoat, choose from matte, satin, or high gloss sealers.

***Supplies pictured at right:***

1. *Latex wall paint*
2. *Colored paint glaze*
3. *Glazing medium, for mixing with latex paint, acrylic craft paint, colored paint glazes, and stencil gel paints*
4. *Acrylic craft paint*
5. *Stencil dry brush paint*
6. *Clear sealer, for sealing raw wood or to use as a topcoat after painting, staining, or glazing*
7. *White primer, for surface preparation and blocking stains*
8. *Spray sealer, to use as a topcoat*
9. *Pump spray antiquing wash*

1.

2.

3.

4.

5.

6.

7.

8.

9.

# BRUSHES & ROLLERS

*You'll need several types of brushes and rollers to create the finishes in this book. Always buy the best quality brush you can afford. Good brushes are a good investment—with proper care, they will last a long time and give you good service. Look for them at paint, hardware, crafts, or art supply stores.*

## • FLAT BRISTLE BRUSHES

These of brushes are used for basecoating walls and furniture. The size you choose depends upon the size of your surface—use wider brushes for painting larger areas and smaller brushes for tighter areas and crevices. **Angled brushes** are used to paint trims and moldings. **Foam brushes** are a handy and inexpensive tool to have for quick repair jobs and for painting furniture.

## • SPECIALTY BRUSHES

Specialty brushes are used to create special effects. The **French brush**, a small, flat brush with short bristles, is used for stippling and creating brushed textures. A **stippler brush**, a flat-ended bristle brush without a handle, is another option for stippling. A **dusting or dragging brush**, sometimes called a "fabric weaver," is a wide brush with short soft bristles and can be used to create textures with the look of woven fabric and to blend colors.

## • STENCIL BRUSHES

Stencil brushes are round bristle brushes with short wooden handles that are designed for stenciling. They are available in a range of sizes. Choose one that's appropriate for the size of the openings in your stencil.

## • ARTIST BRUSHES

Design painting is done with artist's paint brushes. The most common brushes are flats, rounds, and liners. For the designs in this book, rounds are used for applying color, flats are used for blending, and liners are used for detail work. They come in a range of sizes; choose the size according to the size of the design you're painting.

## • PAINT ROLLERS

Paint rollers make quick work of applying paint to flat surfaces. Rollers with short nap create flat finishes; a longer nap creates a slight texture. Smaller rollers are used for smaller areas of walls and for furniture.

## • CLEANING BRUSHES

Thoroughly clean your brushes and rollers after painting to ensure long life and good service. After using latex and waterbase products, wash brushes and rollers with water and a mild soap until all signs of color are gone. Rinse and shake or blot the brush to remove excess water. **Always** allow brushes and rollers to dry before using them again. **Never** use a brush that's been washed and towel dried. If you do, the water that's still in the bristles under the ferrule will come down into the bristles when you stroke and dilute your paint.

Artist's paint brushes and stencil brushes can be cleaned with a commercial brush cleaner. Work the cleaner into the brush and rinse until the water runs clear. Allow to dry.

If you're not using a latex or waterbase paint product, follow the paint manufacturer's instructions for selecting a brush or roller cleaner.

*Supplies pictured at right:*

1. Dusting or dragging brush, sometimes called a "fabric weaver," for blending colors when marbleizing or creating textures on walls.
2. Paint roller with 3/8" nap, for creating slight textures
3. Small brush, for painting corners and crevices
4, 6. Flat brushes, for wall painting
5. Angled brush, for painting trim
7. Small paint roller, for furniture and walls
8, 12. Artist's paint brushes, for design painting
9. Foam brush, for basecoating
10. French brush, for stippling and creating brushed textures
11. Stencil brush, for stenciling

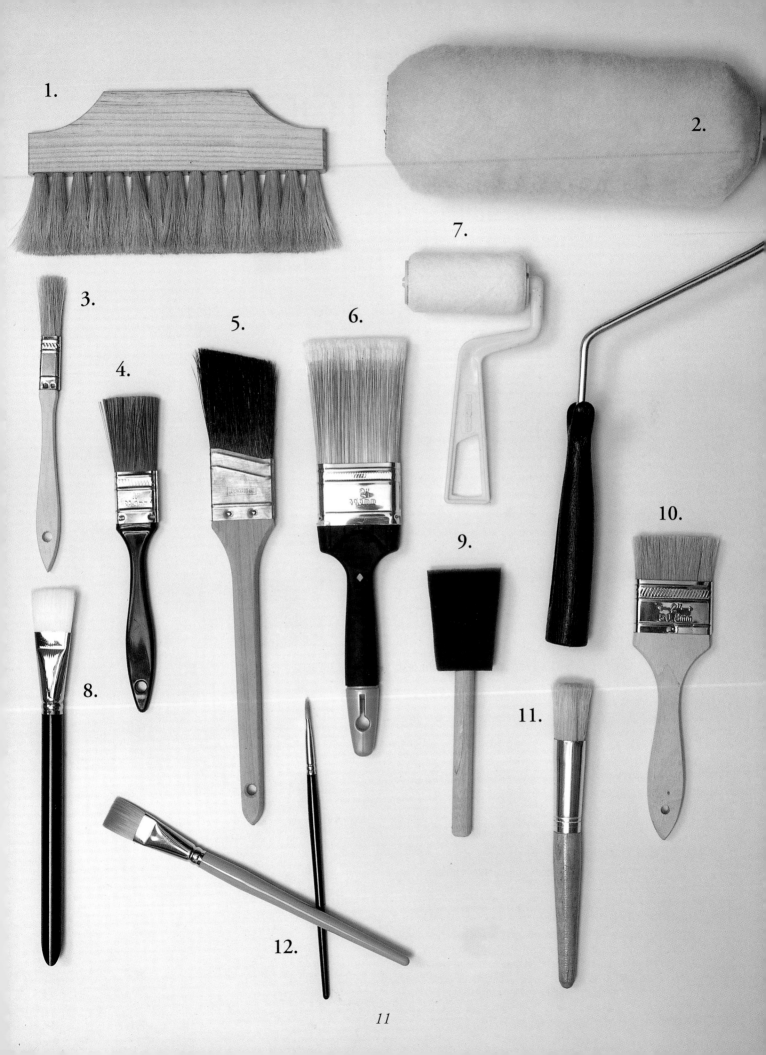

1.

2.

3.

4.

5.

6.

7.

8.

9.

10.

11.

12.

# OTHER TOOLS

*Here are a variety of tools you will need for preparation, or for creating special painted effects.*

## • MEASURING AND MARKING TOOLS

Use a **ruler and pencil** for measuring and marking. Remove marks from surfaces with an **eraser**. To create straight lines, use a spirit level or a plumb line—it's the only way to be sure your lines are straight. Use a **level** to determine true horizontal and vertical lines in a room. A **plumb line**—a string with a weight on one end—can be used to mark a straight line on a wall from top to bottom. After measuring, lines can be marked with a **chalk line**, a gadget that holds a length of coiled string and coats the string with colored chalk.

## • MASKING TAPE

This will become an invaluable material to you when properly used. Use masking tape to mask off moldings and trim so you don't have to worry about getting the wall finish on them. It is also used to mask off borders and stripes. Choose a masking tape that's labeled "low tack." Low tack tape won't leave a residue and is easy to remove.

## • SPONGES

Use **sea sponges** to pounce irregular texture on surfaces and for marbleizing. **Cellulose sponges** can be cut into shapes for stamping designs and are used to apply antiquing and stains to surfaces. Cellulose sponges can also be used for sponging textures on walls, however, they will create a more subtle effect than sea sponges.

## • COMBING TOOLS

**Rubber combs**, for combing and woodgraining, have spaced teeth that cut through glaze mixtures on surfaces, creating patterns and textures.

## • PAINT SCRAPERS

Paint scrapers and putty knives are used to prepare your wall and furniture surfaces by scraping off unwanted paint. They can also be used to create distressed finishes and give the look of aging.

## • SPATTERING TOOLS

Spattering can be done with a specially designed **spatter tool**, which is a mesh screen on a handle (you use a brush to rub paint through the screen). Spattering can also be done with a **toothbrush** or a **nail brush.**

## • COTTON SWABS

Keep some cotton swabs handy for cleaning up small mistakes in finishes.

## • PROTECTIVE GEAR

Be sure to wear a **respirator** or **dust mask** when sanding to protect your mouth and nose from dust. Always work in a well-ventilated area. Latex painters' gloves are inexpensive and help keep your hands clean. Plaster or paper **drop cloths** will protect surrounding areas from paint spills and splatters.

*See the corresponding sections in this book for more information about tools for Aged Plaster, Antiquing, Brushed Textures, Color Washing, Combing and Graining, Crackling, Design Painting, Distressing, Faux Stone, Marbleizing, Ragging, Spattering, and Sponging.*

**Supplies pictured below and at right:**
1, 2. *Respirator and dust mask, to wear when sanding to protect your mouth and nose*
3. *Level*
4. *Ruler, pencil, and eraser, for marking*
5. *Masking tape, in various widths*
6. *Scrapers*
7. *Cotton swabs, for correcting mistakes*
8. *Cellulose and sea sponges*
9. *Rubber comb*
10. *Spatter tool*
11. *Chalk line*
12. *Chalk*
13. *Plumb line*

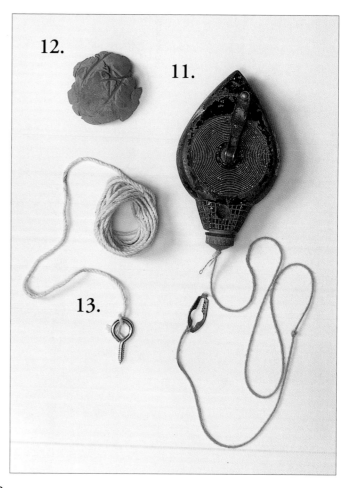

1.

3.

4.

5.

2.

7.

6.

8.

9.

10.

*13*

# SUPPLIES FOR DESIGN PAINTING, STENCILING & STAMPING

*Design painting, stenciling, and stamping are techniques that add decorative motifs to surfaces. For each technique, some specialized tools are required.*

## • DESIGN PAINTING

Patterns for the design painting projects in this book can be enlarged or reduced on a copy machine to accommodate the size of your room or painting surface. **Transfer paper and a pencil** can be used to transfer the design to the surface. Use a variety of **artist's paint brushes** to paint designs.

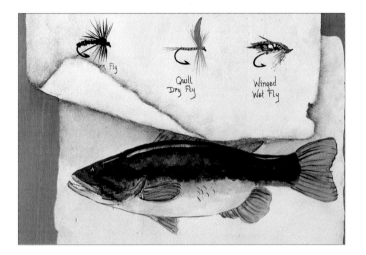

## • STENCILING

Stenciling can be used to create borders and designs on surfaces. A variety of **pre-cut designs** are available or you can cut your own with **blank stencil material**. Secure the stencil to the surface with **masking tape** and apply paint through the openings, using very little paint on the **stencil brush**. When a section is complete, carefully lift the stencil and move it to the next area, using the alignment marks printed or marked on the stencil for proper positioning. When properly cleaned after use, stencils can be used again and again.

**Stencil Design Tape**, another type of pre-cut stencil, is clear tape with designs cut in it and adhesive on the back. Simply press it to the surface and apply paint through the openings. When finished, peel up the tape and discard.

**Acrylic craft paints** and **stencil gel paints** are most often used for stenciling.

### Supplies for Cutting Your Own Stencils:

You can also cut your own stencils. Trace the design on **stencil blank material** with a permanent fine tip marker. Position the stencil blank on a hard cutting surface, such as **a piece of glass** with smooth-finished or taped edges. Cut along the traced lines with a **craft knife**.

## • STAMPING

Stamping is a quick and easy way to add design motifs to surfaces. You simply apply paint onto the face of the stamp, press it to the surface, and lift. Stamping also is called block printing.

A variety of pre-cut stamps, made of foam-type materials, are available at crafts and home improvement centers. They are usually labeled "design stamps" or "printing blocks." You also can cut your own stamps from cellulose sponges or stamping material. Natural materials, such as real leaves or vegetables also may be used.

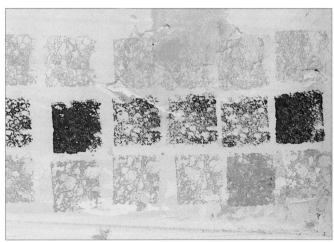

## Supplies for Design Painting, Stenciling & Stamping:

1. Stencil design tape
2. Stencil blank material, for cutting your own stencil
3. Piece of glass with finished edges, to use as a surface when cutting your own stencil
4. Stencil brush
5. Transfer paper and pencil
6. Craft knife, for cutting your own stencils
7. Artist's round brush, for design painting
8. Permanent fine tip marker, for tracing design on stencil blank material before cutting
9. Design stamp, made of foam
10. Design stamps, also called "printing blocks"
11. Real leaves, to use as a design stamp or a pattern for cutting your own stencil
12. Plumb line, for measuring and marking walls for design placement

# PREPARING WALLS

## NEW WALLS

A new wall requires little in the way of preparation. If the wall board or drywall has been sanded smooth, remove dust by brushing or vacuum with the brush attachment of a vacuum cleaner. Apply a painting primer, following manufacturer's instructions.

## OLD WALLS

Remove soil or grease from an old wall by washing the wall with rubbing alcohol, soapy water, or a commercial cleanser meant to be used before painting. If you're using rubbing alcohol or soapy water, rinse the wall thoroughly with clear water and allow to dry. If you're using a commercial cleanser, follow the manufacturer's instructions.

Repair any cracks or holes in the wall with spackling compound, drywall joint compound, or patching plaster, following the package instructions. Allow to dry and sand smooth. An electric sander makes sanding go quicker and easier. Wear a respirator or dust mask and be sure the area is well-ventilated. Remove dust.

Apply primer to patched areas. If you're changing a dark color to a light one, prime the entire wall. If your wall is stained from leaks or wallpaper paste, etc, prime wall to block stains. Let dry.

## BASE PAINTING

The base paint or basecoat is the first color that is applied to the wall and is the foundation for a variety of finishes. Mask off any moldings or trim such as chair rails with low tack masking tape to protect them. Use drop cloths to protect the floor and any furniture that's still in the room. If you're planning to paint the ceiling, paint it before you paint the walls.

You can paint a basecoat with a brush or a short napped roller. When using a brush, use as large a brush as you are comfortable handling and paint with large, sweeping strokes from top to bottom.

When using a roller, you'll first need to use a brush to paint all the areas that you can't easily reach with a roller, such as corners, around moldings, and tight areas. Pour paint in a paint tray, load the roller with paint, and roll on the wall. Use as many coats as are needed to achieve even, opaque coverage. Let dry between coats.

## MAKING A SAMPLE BOARD

Before applying a decorative finish to your wall, do a sample on a piece of poster board or wallboard. A 20" x 30" section would be enough. To make a sample board you should purchase small amounts of your paint colors. Live with the finished piece for a while, studying it in different lights (daylight and artificial light, and at different times of the day). This way, you can be sure you like the colors you've chosen. Making a sample board is also a good way to practice the technique for the finish you've chosen. &

# PREPARING FURNITURE

### NEW FURNITURE

New, unfinished furniture can be found in a variety of styles and types of wood. To prepare the surface, sand thoroughly with medium, then fine sandpaper. *If you're applying a painted finish,* prime the surface with a painting primer. *If you're applying a finish where you want the wood grain to show, such as color washing,* follow individual project instructions regarding sealing and sanding.

Check to see if glue has seeped out around the joints. If it has, it needs to be removed. Either sand away the dried glue or scrape it lightly with a putty knife to remove it.

### OLD FURNITURE

Your own attic, basement, or garage may well hold a piece of old furniture that's suitable for a painted or other faux finish. Tag and yard sales and used furniture and antiques stores are other good sources.

When choosing an old piece to refinish, be sure the piece is in sound condition. If it needs regluing or other work, fix it or have it repaired before applying the finish.

Before finishing, remove all wax, grease, or furniture polish with cleanser, rubbing alcohol, a liquid sandpaper product, or mineral spirits; then sand smooth. Work in a well-ventilated area and wear protective gloves and a dust mask. If the old finish isn't chipped or peeling, sanding may be all that's required. *If you're painting the piece,* use spackling compound to fill unwanted dents, cracks, and holes, let dry, and sand. Wipe away dust with a tack cloth or vacuum. *If you're applying a transparent finish such as a stain,* use a neutral color stainable latex filler. Apply the filler, remove excess while wet, and allow to dry. Sand smooth. If the filler has shrunk during drying, apply more filler, let dry, and sand.

Stripping is necessary if old, peeling paint or varnish can't be sanded smooth or if you want to apply a finish that shows the wood grain. You have two options: take it to a professional or do it yourself. If you decide to strip the piece yourself, choose a stripping agent that is nontoxic and odor free and follow the manufacturer's instructions regarding use, disposal, and protective equipment needed.

### BASE PAINTING

The basecoat is the first coat of the base color, covering the entire surface. The basecoat, usually a satin or eggshell sheen latex paint, is applied with a foam or bristle brush. Use even strokes, leveling out the paint as you work, working in the direction of the wood grain. Allow to dry. Sand the surface with 220 grit sandpaper. Wipe away or vacuum up dust. Apply a second coat and allow to dry. If a third coat is needed, sand, remove dust, and paint again. ❧

# COLOR STAINING WOOD

*Color staining imparts vibrant color to wood but—unlike paint—allows the grain and natural beauty of the wood to show through the color. Color staining can be rubbed or brushed on walls, ceilings, and floors to impart overall color effects or designs can be stenciled or painted with stain to create faux inlay patterns on any wood surface.*

## SUPPLIES

A variety of premixed products can be used for color staining, but it's also easy to create your own custom colors.

Premixed products include **wood stains**, available in brown and jewel tones, and **spray-on color washes**, which are waterbase colors in spray bottles.

You can create your own stains by mixing neutral **glazing medium** with **latex wall or trim paint, paint glaze,** or **acrylic craft paint.** Neutral glazing medium is usually packaged in large tubs such as this 48 oz. size shown and package instructions give suggested proportions for mixing. You'll need a **stir stick** for mixing the color stain. For floors, oil paint can be diluted with paint thinner to make a stain. Oil paint penetrates into the wood deeper and allows for more wear and tear.

Color stains that you buy or mix yourself can be applied with a **sponge** or brushed on the surface with **bristle or sponge brushes.** Have some clean, soft **cloth rags** on hand for wiping off excess color stain and for buffing surfaces.

**Supplies Pictured for Color Staining Wood:**

1. Glazing medium, neutral
2. Spray-on color wash, premixed
3. Colored paint glaze, option for tinting glazing medium
4, 5. Acrylic craft paint, option for tinting glazing medium
6. Wood stain, premixed

7. Stir stick
8. Sponge, option for applying color stain
9, 10, 11. Bristle and sponge brushes, option for applying color stain
12. Rag, for wiping excess stain

## HERE'S HOW

### COLORWAYS

#### 1

In a disposable container, mix 3 parts glazing medium with 1 part paint glaze, acrylic paint, or latex paint. This will give you a wash consistency. You will always want to experiment with your proportions to obtain the intensity of color you desire. Mix small amounts first and apply to a scrap piece of wood. After you have the correct proportions, you can then mix larger amounts of glaze mixture.

#### 2

Brush mixture on surface, working in the direction of the wood grain. Use brushes or sponges as pictured, choosing the tool that is most comfortable for you.

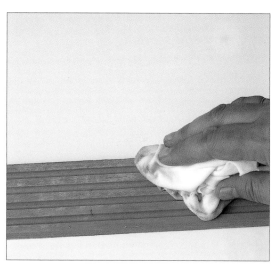

#### 3

Wipe off excess with a soft cloth, rubbing in the direction of the wood grain. This will give a more even coverage. If you have a very thin mixture, wiping it off may not be necessary. Test your technique on a scrap piece of wood first.

*Glazing medium + white latex paint*

*Glazing medium + blue gel paint*

*Premixed walnut wood stain*

# STAINED WALLS & CEILING

*The natural colors of sea, sky, and shore that surround this lake house supplied the inspiration for its decor. The use of color creates seamless transitions from inside to outdoors and echoes the glorious views from the windows and the deck. Color staining was used to tone and soften the wooden walls and ceilings, with beautiful results.*

## 1
### Supplies

**Paint and Medium:**
> Blue latex wall paint
> White latex wall paint
> Neutral Glazing medium

*Measure the room to determine how much paint and glazing medium to buy. You'll need enough glazing medium to cover the square footage of the walls and ceiling combined. Purchase about 1/3 the amount of paint you'd need if you were painting the walls and ceiling.*

**Tools & Equipment:**
> Drop cloth
> Sandpaper
> Ladder
> Masking tape
> Bristle brush
> Cellulose sponge
> Rag or cloth
> Dust mask or respirator
> *Optional:* Electric sander

## 2
### Preparation

Wearing a dust mask, sand the walls and ceiling. Vacuum up the dust.

## 3
### Color Staining the Walls

1. Mask off the walls to protect the ceiling and floors from the stain.
2. Mix glazing medium and white latex paint, using 3 parts glazing medium and 1 part paint. Test the mixture on a scrap of wood to be sure it's to your liking. You do not want the wood to look painted; you want to see the wood grain. Add more paint if you'd like a more opaque look, more glazing medium if you'd like more transparency. If the mixture seems too thick, add 1-2 teaspoons of water to thin.
3. Apply the glazing mixture with a bristle brush, brushing it evenly over the surface. Working one board or panel at a time, complete an entire board or panel; then move on to the next. Rub with a soft rag or a moist sponge to smooth out the color here and there. Remove tape. Allow to dry.

## 4
### Color Staining the Ceiling

1. Mask off the ceiling to protect the walls.
2. Mix glazing medium and blue latex paint, using 3 parts glazing medium and 1 part paint. Again, test the mixture on a scrap of wood to be sure it's to your liking and add more paint if you'd like a more opaque look, more glazing medium if you'd like more transparency. If the mixture seems to thick, add 1-2 teaspoons of water to thin.
3. Apply the glazing mixture with a bristle brush, brushing it evenly over the surface. Working one board or panel at a time, complete an entire board or panel; then move on to the next. Rub with a soft rag or a moist sponge to smooth out the color here and there. Allow to dry. Remove tape.

## 5
### Finishing

Lightly buff the wood with sandpaper for a smooth finish if color staining has raised the grain of the wood. 🎗

# FAUX INLAY CONSOLE TABLE

*Color staining was used to create a faux inlay look on this simple wooden table. The stained design was stenciled, using stenciling tape and three colors of gel stencil paint. A light stain on the entire table gives a mellow look.*

## 1
### Supplies

**Surface:** Wooden console table

**Stencil:** Egg and Dart design in 4" stencil
tape

**Paint and Finishes:**
Walnut wood stain or antiquing
Black wood stain or antiquing
Honey gold wood stain or antiquing
Natural wood stain
Waterbase varnish

**Tools & Equipment:**
Masking tape
Stencil brushes - one for each color
Foam brush
Rag
Ruler
Tack cloth
Pencil

## 2
### Preparation

1. Sand surface until smooth. Wipe away dust with a tack cloth.
2. Position stenciling tape on the surface, using project photos as a guide for placement. Be sure to leave room for the outer stripes and to position the tape in such a way that the design motifs will fit nicely in the corners. The stenciling tape, which is a clear, adhesive-backed tape with the design cut into it, can be repositioned. *If you're using a stencil,* make paper proofs to ensure proper positioning.

## 3
### Stenciling

1. Using photos as a guide for color placement, stencil the design with walnut, honey gold, and black wood stains or antiquing **(photo 1)**. Work with a nearly dry brush to prevent run-unders, and use a different brush for each color. Allow to dry. To deepen the color, reapply the stain. Allow to dry. Remove the stenciling tape **(photo 2)**.
2. Mask off a stripe around the design on the tabletop and around the apron of the table. Stain with walnut. Remove tape and allow to dry.
3. Mask off a narrow stripe on the tabletop outside of the walnut stripe and stain with black. Remove tape and allow to dry.

## 4
### Finishing

1. Apply natural wood stain to the entire table. Allow to dry.
2. Seal the surface with 1-3 coats waterbase varnish. Allow to dry between coats. ✿

Photo 1

Photo 2

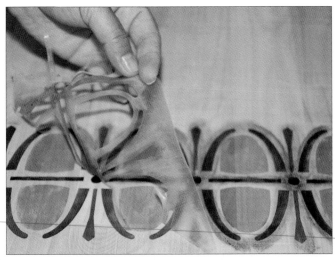

# FAUX INLAY STAINED FLOOR

*In this living room, a floral design was color stained on the floor to create the look of an inlaid border. The heart pine floor was not in perfect condition, so before the border was applied, it was repaired and sanded, and a wood-tone stain was applied to the entire floor to even out the color. The design can be hand painted with an artist's brush or stenciled. In the photos here we show the hand painting technique*

## 1
## Supplies

**Paints and Finishes:**
  Oil-base or waterbase wood-tone stain
  Dark brown tube oil paint
  Light brown tube oil paint
  Dark green tube oil paint
  Deep red tube oil paint
  Paint thinner
  Polyurethane floor sealer or tung oil finish

**Tools & Equipment:**
  Artist's paint brush - #8 round
  Tracing paper
  Transfer paper
  Tape measure or ruler
  Pencil
  Chalk line and red chalk powder
  Disposable cups
  Low tack masking tape
  Cloth rags
  Rubber gloves
  *Optional:* Sponge mop

## 2
## Preparation

1. Hire a professional to sand the floor or do it yourself with a floor sander. Vacuum up the dust.
2. Apply the wood-tone stain to the floor. (I used a sponge mop to apply the stain **(photo 1)**.) Allow to dry according to package instructions.
3. Measure 3" from the wall and tape off a stripe 1-1/2" wide. Tape off a second 1-1/2" stripe 21" from the wall **(photo 2)**. Use a pencil to mark the measurements and a chalk line to mark the lines for taping.
4. Enlarge the patterns for this project on a copy machine.
5. Trace the photocopied design on tracing paper. Tape the tracing paper to the floor. Slip transfer paper between the floor and the tracing paper. Go over the lines to transfer the pattern to the floor **(photo 3)**.

## 3
## *Color Staining*

1. Using a separate cup for each paint color, dilute each paint color with paint thinner to make a transparent stain, using 3 parts paint to 1 part thinner. Test the mixtures on a scrap of wood before applying the color stain to your floor.
2. Stain the stripes with dark brown **(photo 4)**. *NOTE: Some of the floral design overlaps the taped stripes. When you stain the stripes, be sure to leave a 1/4" space between the design and the stripe.* Allow to dry. Remove tape.
3. Paint the floral design with light brown, dark green, and deep red. Use photos as guides for color placement. Be sure to stroke the color enough to get a transparent look **(photo 5)**. Allow to dry.

## 4
## *Finishing*

Apply polyurethane OR a tung oil finish to the floor, brushing over design quickly and working small sections at a time. 🐝

**Before**

1

2

3

4

5

## After

*Use this photo for your pattern. Trace from book and enlarge to desired size.*

*Trace pattern from book and enlarge to desired size for corners.*

# MARBLEIZING

*Marbleizing—the technique of applying paint to surfaces to create the look of marble—has been a popular substitute for real marble for centuries. Faux marble can be created on any paintable surface, including walls, woodwork, and furniture, but it's especially popular for fireplace mantles. The following pages show three rooms where marbleized finishes have been used and tell you how to create them.*

## SUPPLIES

Faux marble designs are created by mingling several **paint** colors on a surface. A number of types of acrylic paint can be used such as acrylic craft paint, latex wall paint, or gel stenciling paint, or paint glaze. Before they are applied to the surface, the paints are mixed with **neutral glazing medium** to increase the drying time and make them easier to blend. A number of tools, including **stippler brushes, French brushes, and cellulose and sea sponges,** can be used to apply the paint colors. A wide, **soft bristle brush** called the "fabric weaver" is used to smooth and blend colors. **Feathers** are used to create the marble's veins and cracks.

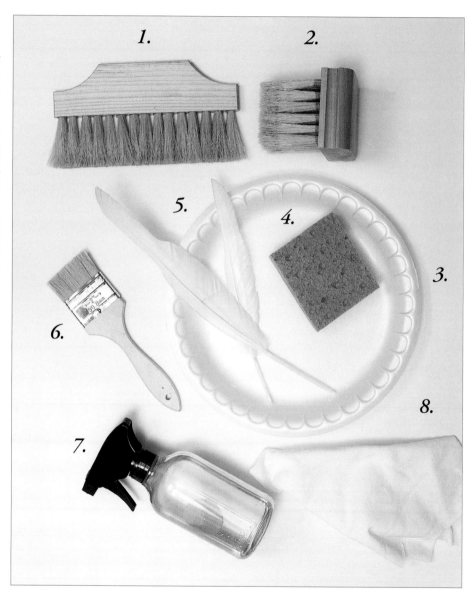

### *Tools Pictured for Marbleizing:*

1. *Wide, soft brush (called a "fabric weaver"), for smoothing and blending*
2. *Stippler brush (a square, flat ended brush, 3" x 3"), for applying paint*
3. *Disposable plate, used as a palette*
4. *Cellulose sponge, for applying paint to surface*
5. *Feathers, for creating veining and cracks in marble*
6. *French brush, for pouncing paint on surface*
7. *Spray bottle of water, for spritzing surface to keep paint moist and workable for blending*
8. *Rag, for wiping feathers, brushes, etc.*

## TIPS FOR CREATING REALISTIC VEINS AND CRACKS

- When a crack intersects a vein, pick up the feather, and reposition it on the other side of the vein, either up or down, and continue. Fissure cracks do not look like Xs, Ys, or Zs and they do not stay parallel; they shift up or down slightly.
- When you pull the veins and cracks, slightly shake your hand to create milky, wavy lines. They will look more natural. (That's why a feather works better than an artist's liner brush—because you have less control over the feather.)
- The veins should have wide and narrow areas, and the color should be deeper in some areas than in others. Most of the drifts and veins are parallel, but some are not.
- Create as many drifts, veins, and cracks as you like—real marble has areas with no veining and other areas that look almost white because they have so many veins.

## HERE'S HOW

*1*

*2*

Using a separate container for each color, mix each paint color with neutral glazing medium. Coat surface to be marbleized with glazing medium. The glazing medium wets the surface and allows the colors to move softly and mingle **(photo 1)**. Pounce first color glaze mixture (here, green) on some areas of the surface with stippler brush to create a drift of color **(photo 2)**. Wipe brush onto damp cloth.

*3*

*4*

Pounce second color glaze mixture (here, peach) with stippler brush. The idea is to create distinct drifts of color, not to mix the colors together. Allow to dry **(photo 3)**. To create veins, dip the tip of the feather (about 1-1/2") in white paint. Holding the feather as a violinist holds a bow, paint the veins with the feather as you nervously shake your hand while pulling the feather **(photo 4)**.

*5*

*6*

Drag the fabric weaver brush to blend colors slightly and feather out veins **(photo 5)**. Again with the feather, create the fissure cracks. Pull the tip of the feather through the white, and then pull a very slight crack onto the surface **(photo 6)**.

# TRADITIONAL FIREPLACE & WAINSCOTTING PANELS

*In the 19th century, itinerant craftsmen traveled the countryside creating a variety of faux finishes for well-to-do farmers. Today, the parlor of this elegant country farm house echoes earlier times with a marbleized mantle and wall panels that stand out against the white trim of the wainscotting. The colors chosen for the faux marble blend with the terra cotta tones of the brick hearth and the floral patterned rug.*

*See closeup of room on page 127.*

## 1
## Supplies

**Paints and Finishes:**

Antique white latex wall paint, satin finish

Deep peach latex wall paint

Linen white latex wall paint

Metallic gold acrylic craft paint

Sage green latex wall paint

Neutral glazing medium

Matte or high gloss waterbase varnish or polyurethane

**Tools & Equipment:**

Foam or bristle brush and paint roller for applying basecoat

Stippler brush

French brush

Fabric weaver brush

Spray bottle filled with water

Masking tape

Feather

Disposable plates

Clean, soft cloth rag

## 2
## Preparation

1. Mask off areas to be marbleized.
2. Paint each area to be marbleized with 1-2 coats Antique White. Allow to dry between coats. Let final coat dry thoroughly.

## 3
## Marbleizing

*Work one area at a time so you will be able to blend the glaze mixtures slightly before they dry out. From time to time, as needed, use a spray bottle to spritz the surface to keep the glaze mixtures moist. The colors should look blended and mellow, but not muddy.*

**Mix and apply colors:**

1. Using a separate container for each color, mix equal amounts of glazing medium and sage green, deep peach, metallic gold, and linen white. Pour each of the colors on a clean plate or paint tray. Dampen a cloth.
2. Brush or roll a coat of glazing medium on the surface.
3. Dip the tips of the stippler brush in the linen white glaze mixture and work the color on the surface. Wipe the stippler brush bristles with the damp cloth.
4. Dip the brush bristles in the sage green glaze mixture and apply random drifts of color to the surface. Wipe the bristles again.
5. Apply the deep peach glaze mixture. Wipe the bristles again.
6. Randomly apply the metallic gold glaze mixture. Allow to dry.
7. Repeat steps 2-6 until all areas are finished. Allow to dry.

**Add veins and cracks:**

*Again, work one area at a time.*

8. Mix 1 part glazing medium with 4 parts white paint. Dip the tip (about 1-1/2") of the feather in the diluted paint and drag and pull the feather over the surface to create veins. If the paint seems too thick, add a couple of drops of water to the mix.
9. Before the white glaze mixture dries out, brush the veins lightly with the fabric weaver brush to blend and soften. Allow to dry completely.
10. Again using the tip of your feather and the white glaze mixture, go back over some of the veins to create a more vivid look. Have a few more pronounced veins to contrast with your soft, blended look.
11. Adjacent to the vein lines, use the tip of the feather to create cracks. Pick up the tip of the feather and reposition it either slightly above or slightly below on the other side of the vein so it looks as if the marble has cracked and slightly shifted. Allow to dry.

## 4
## Finishing

Seal the surface with a matte sealer for the look of low sheen, low-buffed marble or with a high gloss sealer for a high-buffed appearance. 🎀

# VICTORIAN MANTLE AND MIRROR

*For the marbleizing on this mantle and mirror frame, the paint is applied with a sponge. Using a sponge creates the scaly look of serpentine marble—so called because the surface of the stone resembles snakeskin.*

## 1
## *Supplies*

**Latex Wall Paint and Finishes:**
Black, flat or satin sheen
Deep green
Medium olive green
White
Glazing medium
High gloss varnish or polyurethane

**Tools & Equipment:**
2 cellulose sponges
Foam brush
Bristle brush
*Optional:* Small paint roller
Feather
Disposable plates
Sandpaper, 220 grit
Tack cloth or soft cloth

## 2
## *Preparation*

1. Sand areas to be marbleized. Wipe away dust.
2. Basecoat with 1-3 coats of black latex paint. Allow to dry.
3. Moisten the cellulose sponges. Cut one sponge in a wedge shape (for working in the tight crevices of the mantle and mirror frame). Pinch and tear small pieces from the straight edges and surfaces of the sponges. (They should resemble Swiss cheese.)

## 3
## *Marbleizing*

**Mix and apply colors:**
1. In individual containers, mix an equal amount of glazing medium with dark green, medium green, and white paint.
2. Use a spoon or a stir stick to drizzle circles of the dark green color and medium green glaze mixtures on a disposable plate. Add a couple of dots of white glaze mixture. Don't mix the colors—you don't want them blended.
3. Dip the dampened sponge in the drizzled paints. Place the sponge on the surface, lightly press, pick up, change positions, and press again. Repeat the process until all areas are complete, reloading sponge as needed. Allow to dry.

- Rinse and clean your sponge often to prevent the colors from mingling on the sponge.
- When the drizzled paint on the plate starts to look muddy or blended, discard or clean the plate you are using and drizzle on fresh paint as you did in Step 1.
- Don't use too much white.

**Add veins and cracks:**
4. Use the feather with the white glaze mixture to pull veins and cracks across the surface. (You will be able to see the sponged colors through the veins and cracks.) Allow to dry thoroughly.

## 4
## *Finishing*

Apply high gloss, water-base or oil-base varnish or polyurethane, brush on or spray on. If you want a dull and not a high gloss, buffed appearance, use a matte finish. ❦

*Closeup of Victorian Mantle*

# White & Black
# Marbleized Fireplace & Woodwork

# • WHITE & BLACK MARBLEIZED FIREPLACE & WOODWORK •

*This traditional, formal mantle combines white marbleizing and black marbleizing for drama and contrast. A white faux marble finish was also applied to the chair rail.*

*Before*

*Instructions for ragged
wall treatment on page 46.*

# WHITE & BLACK
# MARBLEIZIED FIREPLACE & WOODWORK

## 1
## *Supplies*

**Latex Wall Paint and Finishes:**
 White, satin sheen
 Oyster white
 Tan
 Mushroom
 Black, satin sheen
 Glazing medium
 Waterbase varnish or polyurethane,
  satin finish

**Tools & Equipment:**
 Stippler brush
 French brush
 2" trim brush
 Low tack masking tape
 Disposable plates
 2 paint trays
 Rag
 Feather
 Sea sponge
 Spray bottle filled with water
 *Optional:* Spattering tool or old tooth-
  brush

## 2
## *Preparation*

Paint chair rail and areas of mantle with white-background marble with white paint. Paint columns and inset, base molding and crown molding, with black paint. Use as many coats as necessary to achieve good coverage. Allow to dry between coats. Let final coat dry completely.

## 3
## *White Marbleizing*

**Mix and apply colors:**
1. Using a separate container for each color, mix oyster white paint and tan paint with equal amounts of glazing medium. Pour 1 cup oyster white glaze mixture in one paint tray. Pour 1 cup tan glaze mixture in other paint tray.
2. Using the stippler brush with the oyster white glaze and the French brush with the tan glaze, simultaneously pounce the colors on the surfaces to create drifts of color. Continue until all surfaces are complete. Allow to dry.

**Add veins and spatter:**
3. Mix small amounts of tan and oyster white glaze mixtures. Put about 1 teaspoon of this mixture on a disposable plate. Using the feather, create veins.
4. With the tip of the feather and the same glaze mix, create cracks. Allow to dry.
5. *Optional:* Using the spattering tool or a toothbrush with the tan glaze mixture, spatter the surface randomly. For more about spattering, see "Spattering" section. Allow to dry completely.

## 4
## *Black Marbleizing*

**Mix and apply colors:**
1. Mask off areas to receive the black marbleizing.
2. Mix 5 parts glazing medium with 1 part white paint. Drizzle lines of the glaze mixture on a clean disposable plate. Dampen the sea sponge. Squeeze out excess water.
3. Press sponge in white glaze on plate, then press and pat sponge on black-painted surfaces. The white sponging should look milky and transparent. If an area looks too bright, use a spray bottle filled with water to spritz it—this will dilute the glaze and mellow the intensity. Allow to dry.

**Add veins and cracks:**
4. Use the feather to create subtle vein and crack lines. Allow to dry.

## 5
## *Finishing*

Brush several coats of waterbase varnish or polyurethane over the surfaces to protect them. ❧

# FAUX STONES

*A concrete wall at the back of an alcove in this ground floor family room was transformed with paint and brushes to look like a stacked stone wall—with fabulous results. It became the perfect place for a wine cellar.*

*Before you begin, study the color and design of real stone walls and photographs of stone walls. You can also take pictures of a wall that appeals to you and use them as guides for your faux stone wall.*

## SUPPLIES

The faux stone finish is created by covering a wall with **adhesive-backed clear plastic.** The stone shapes, cut from **cardboard,** are traced on the plastic with a **fine tip marker** and cut out with a **craft knife.** A **stencil** may also be used. Paint colors for the stones are mixed with glazing medium. A **paint roller or sponge brush** is used to randomly apply the background colors to the stone shapes. More layers of color are added to create realistic variation, using the **French brush,** a **stencil brush,** or a **sea sponge.** It's handy to have a **spray bottle filled with water** nearby to spritz the wall lightly as you work to keep the glaze mixtures from drying out too quickly. An **artist's paint brush** adds the finishing touches of painted mortar between the stone shapes.

### Supplies Pictured for Faux Stone:

1. Clear adhesive-backed plastic, for creating a stencil for the faux stone
2. Fine tip permanent marker, for tracing the stone shapes
3. Craft knife, for cutting the stencil
4. Stone shapes cut from cardboard
5. Cobblestone pre-cut stencil design can be used as an option
6. Paint roller, for painting background colors
7. French brush, for applying glaze mixtures
8. Foam brush, for painting background color on wall
9. Artist's paint brush, for painting mortar between stone shapes
10. Stencil brush, for applying glaze mixtures to create stone textures
11. Sea sponge, for applying glaze mixtures to create stone textures
12. Spray bottle filled with water, for spritzing wall while working to keep glaze moist and workable

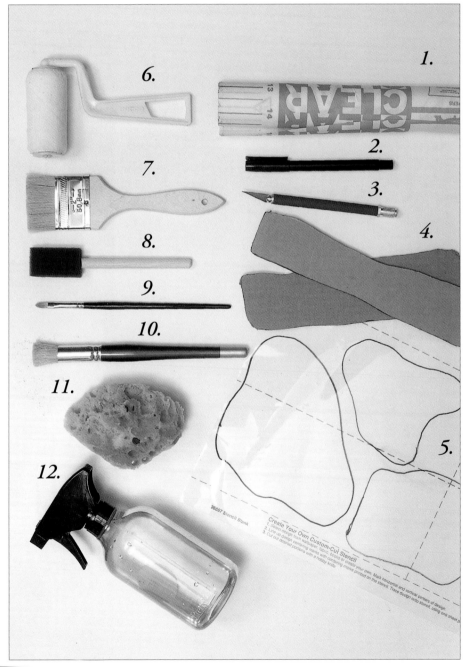

**See Step-by-Step photos and instructions on pages 40 & 41.**

# Stacked Stone Wine Cellar

## 1
## *Supplies*

**Latex Wall Paint:**
Cream
Tan
Gray
Dark gray
*Optional:* Light gray, for basecoat (In this instance, the gray color of the concrete is the "basecoat," and the light gray paint isn't necessary.)

**Other Supplies:**
Glazing medium
Clear adhesive-backed plastic, enough to cover the wall
Options: Pre-cut stencil with stone pattern or stencil blank material to cut a stacked stone pattern or low tack masking tape. (If you use a stencil or tape, you don't need adhesive backed paper.)

**Tools & Equipment:**
2 foam brushes
French brush
Artist's paint brush
Sea sponge or sea sponging mitt
Black permanent marker
Spray bottle filled with water
Craft knife
Pieces of cardboard
Drop cloth
Ladder

## 2
## *Creating the Pattern*

1. Cut lengths of adhesive-backed plastic the width of the wall. Remove the backing paper and gently press the adhesive side to the wall **(photo 1)**.
2. Cut 5 or 6 stone shapes from cardboard—some elongated, some fatter and more square.
3. Hold the shapes against the adhesive-backed plastic on the wall and trace around them with a permanent marker **(photo 2)**. Repeat until the wall is covered with the shapes. (The pattern is similar to that of brick, but less regular.)
4. With a craft knife, cut around each of the marked stones and gently remove the plastic film inside the stone shape, leaving thin pieces or bridges of plastic. The bridges are the mortar between the stones.
5. Firmly press the bridges to the wall so the paint won't bleed under them.

## 3
## *Applying the Paint*

1. In separate containers, mix each paint color with glazing medium, using three parts paint and one part glazing medium.

*The more randomly you place the colors, the more realistic your wall will look. For a more weathered appearance when stippling or sponging, lightly mist the surface with water as you work the different paint colors. Do not spray heavily or your paint will run and the adhesive-backed paper could come loose.*

2. Randomly paint stones with cream, tan, and gray paint mixtures. You don't have to cover the gray background completely. (It won't look a lot like stone at this point.) Allow to dry.
3. Dip the tips of the bristle brush in the dark gray and stipple the wall **(photo 3)**. Stipple some stones heavily, so only a little of the base coloring shows. Stipple others lightly, so more of the base coloring shows. Don't try to make them look alike. Wipe the bristle brush with a damp cloth. (Don't clean the brush with water—if you do, the water that remains in the shank of the brush will dilute the paint.)
4. Dip the wiped-off brush in the terra cotta color. Randomly stipple the color on a few pieces, allowing the background colors to show through.
5. Add more dark gray and mingle the colors for a realistic look.
6. Moisten the sea sponge or sea sponging mitt. Dip sponge or mitt in the cream paint mixture and lightly press, pounce, and pat the color over the stones **(photo 4)**. (You're not trying to create a sponged finish, you're adding more texture.) Sponge some stones more than others.
7. Step back and look at the stones. Add more of any color, stippling or sponging the paint mixture(s) on the wall.
8. When the stones are as you want them, gently remove all of the pieces of adhesive-backed paper **(photo 5)**.

## 4
## *Painting the Mortar*

Use an artist's brush with charcoal gray paint to paint the recessed mortar **(photo 6)**. Don't completely surround each stone; randomly stroke around here and there, sometimes an entire edge, sometimes not. The mortar around some stones should look darker than the mortar around others.

## 5
## *Finishing*

When the paint is dry, it's finished. I don't use a sealer on faux stone—even a matte sealer imparts a sheen, and any sheen makes the surface look less realistic. 🐝

## HERE'S HOW

*1*

*2*

*3*

*4*

*5*

*6*

# RAGGING

*An array of wonderful wall textures can be created with colored glazes. Textured walls can enhance any room, and they add interest to any decorating style. The following pages show the techniques for creating ragged, sponged, and brushed textures.*

## SUPPLIES

Ragging and rag rolling involve the application of a **glaze mixture** over a painted basecoat. The glaze takes on the texture of what's used to apply it—options include **cloth rags and a ragging mitt**, which is a cloth mitt with loops of fabric attached to its face. Another type of texture can be created with plastic sheeting.

The glaze is made by combining a **neutral glazing medium** with **acrylic craft paint, colored paint glaze, or latex paint**. Use a **stir stick** to mix the glaze.

### Supplies Pictured for Ragging:

1. *Glazing medium, neutral*
2. *Colored paint glaze, for mixing with glazing medium*
3. *Acrylic craft paint, for mixing with glazing medium*
4. *Stir stick*
5, 6. *Rag options for ragging*
7. *Ragging mitt*
8. *Plastic drop cloth, for creating another texture*

*See Step-by-Step photos and instructions on page 44.*

## HERE'S HOW — USING A MITT

### 1

Mix paint with glazing medium. Dampen mitt with water and squeeze out excess.

### 2

Pour glaze mixture in a paint tray. Load mitt by pouncing face of mitt in glaze mixture. Blot the face of the mitt on the grid of the paint tray to distribute the color.

### 3

Pounce mitt on surface, changing hand position frequently. Reload mitt as needed. From time to time, rinse glaze mixture from mitt, blot, and reload.

## HERE'S HOW — USING RAGS

### 1

Dip rag in paint glaze to saturate. Blot rag, crumple, and shape into a roll.

### 2

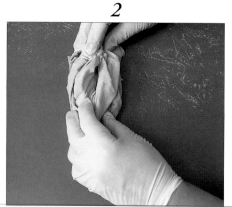

Roll rag on wall, up and down and back and forth. Repeat procedure to complete walls.

## RAG ROLLED BEDROOM WALLS

### 1
### Supplies

**Latex Wall Paint and Medium:**
   Purple, satin sheen
   Lavender
   Glazing medium

**Tools & Equipment:**
   Bristle brush and/or paint roller
   Ragging mitt or rags
   Disposable paint tray, Latex gloves
   Bucket, Ladder, Drop cloth
   Low tack masking tape

### 2
### Preparation

*The ceiling in this room was color stained with a mixture of glazing medium and white paint. See section on "Color Staining Wood" for instructions.*

1. Prepare walls. Mask off moldings with tape.
2. Paint walls with 2-3 coats purple latex paint. (A color this deep requires more coats than a lighter color.) Allow to dry thoroughly according to manufacturer's instructions.
3. Mix glazing medium and lavender paint, using 3 parts glazing medium and 1 part paint.

### 3
### Ragging

*Test the colors on a scrap of wood or a piece of cardboard before ragging your walls. Simply paint the board the basecoat color, let it dry, and apply some of the glaze mixture with the ragging mitt or rags. To make the ragging color lighter, add more glazing medium. To darken, add more paint. Practice your ragging technique so the surface won't look striped, smudged, or overlapped. Wear latex gloves to protect your hands.*

Rag walls according to instructions given for using a mitt or using rags.

# RAGGED & TEXTURED WALL

*The walls in this room use two ragging techniques to create rich texture. After being painted a medium green color, the lower walls were coated with a thick coat of dark green glaze. Pieces of plastic sheeting (such as that used for plastic drop cloths) were applied over the glaze, pressed, and lifted to create another ragged texture.*

*The upper walls were painted with textured paint. The same glaze mixture used on the lower walls was brushed on, then rubbed and patted with a ragging mitt.*

## 1
## *Supplies*

**Paint and Mediums:**
Medium green latex wall paint, satin sheen
Glazing medium
Dark green latex paint or colored paint
    glaze
Texture medium (available in paint depart-
    ments and paint stores)

**Tools & Equipment:**
    Paint roller and roller cover with 1/2"
      nap
    2 paint trays
    2" or 3" bristle paint brush
    Low tack masking tape
    Sandpaper, 120 grit
    Ragging mitt
    Plastic drop cloths, 1 mil thick

**(Photo at right)**
**Closeup of wall texture**
**See page 34 for an overall view of the room.**

## 2
## *Preparation*

1. Prepare walls. Tape around moldings with low tack tape.
2. Apply texture medium to upper walls according to manufacturer's instructions. *If the texture medium you purchased is a paint additive,* add it to the medium green wall paint and paint the upper walls. Allow to dry.
3. Paint the upper and lower walls with 1-2 coats medium green latex paint. Allow to dry between coats.
4. Mix glazing medium and dark green paint or paint glaze, using 3 parts glazing medium and 1 part paint or colored glaze.

## 3
## *Upper Walls*

1. Dampen the ragging mitt and squeeze out excess water. Blot the face of the mitt on a dry terry towel.
2. Brush or pounce the glaze mixture on the upper walls with a bristle brush, working one small (about 3' x 3') area at a time, and then pat and rub the glaze with the mitt to make an uneven, irregular pattern. Be sure not to work in squares but in irregular shapes so the places where you stop and start won't show. Continue until all areas have been glazed and worked with the mitt. Rinse and blot the mitt as needed. Allow to dry overnight.
3. *Optional:* Lightly sand the wall for an aged, distressed look. Wipe away dust.

## 4
## *Lower Walls*

1. Cut the plastic drop cloth into pieces approximately 20" x 30".
2. Working one area at a time, roll a thick coat of glaze on the lower wall (**photo 1**) and, while the glaze is still wet, press the plastic on the surface and lightly pat and rub (**photo 2**). Wrinkles will form in the plastic and create a crinkled, mottled effect in the glaze. Carefully remove the plastic (**photo 3**).
3. Continue with remaining areas and pieces of plastic, using a fresh piece of plastic in each area for best results. Allow to dry. ✤

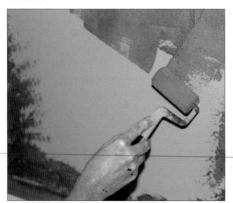

*Photo 1*

*Photo 2*

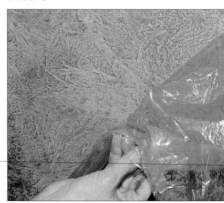

*Photo 3*

# SPONGING

*A sponging technique applied to walls and furniture gives a mottled look, adding interest to the surface. Sponging is a simple, quick technique that uses a sponge to create texture with glaze on a painted surface. The final effect depends on the sponge used.*

## SUPPLIES

A variety of sponge types can be used to apply a colored glazing mixture to the walls. Sponge options include **natural or sea sponges, cellulose household sponges, and sponging mitts** (a cellulose or sea sponge attached to a cloth mitt). The colored glaze mixture for sponging is made by combining a **neutral glazing medium** with **acrylic craft paint, colored paint glaze, or latex paint**. Use a **stir stick** to mix the glaze in a disposable container.

### Supplies Pictured for Sponging:

1. *Glazing medium, neutral*
2. *Colored paint glaze option for mixing with glazing medium*
3. *Acrylic craft paint, option for mixing with glazing medium*
4. *Latex wall paint, option for mixing with glazing medium*
5. *Stir stick*
6. *Cellulose sponge, option for applying glaze mixture*
7. *Sea sponge, option for applying glaze mixture*
8. *Sponging mitt, option for applying glaze mixture*
9. *Sea sponging mitt, option for applying glaze mixture*

# HERE'S HOW

## 1

Mix paint and glazing medium. Dampen sponge. Squeeze out excess water.

## 2

Pour some of the glaze mixture in a paint tray. Dip sponge in glaze mixture to saturate sponge with glaze. Pounce sponge on surface.

## 3

Measure walls and mark stripes, using a plumb line and masking tape. Tape along the outside of the marked lines for the stripes to be sponged. Pounce loaded sponge on surface between taped lines. Allow to dry. Remove tape.

# SPONGED &
# STRIPED
# BEDROOM

*Before*

*The photo above left shows the room before renovation. The photo above right shows the room after the wallpaper had been stripped.*

*(Photo on page 51)*
*\* Instructions for Faux Inlay Console Table can be found in "Color Staining" section.*

*\* A closeup of the Crackled Campaign Chest can be found in the "Crackling" section.*

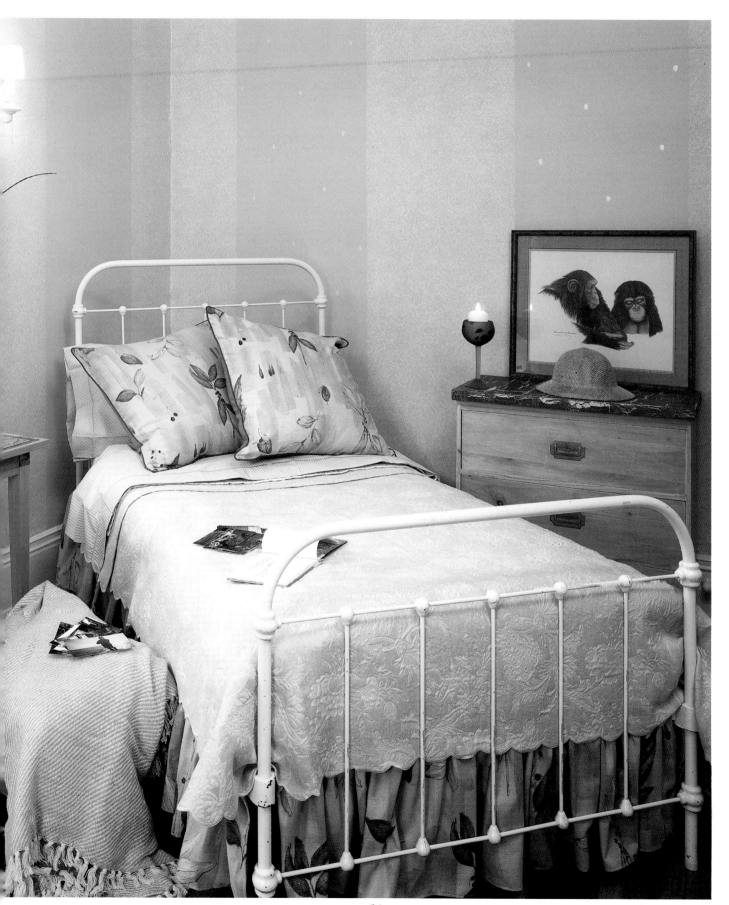

# SPONGED & STRIPED BEDROOM

*The soothing natural colors of this guest room would make any traveler feel at peace. Taupe and ivory were used for walls and bed linens, creating a monochromatic color scheme. Small touches of dark red and olive green are used as accents.*

*The walls were painted taupe. Linen white was used to paint the woodwork and to tint the glaze used for sponging the stripes. The metallic fingerprint dots on the taupe stripes are simple to do and give a whimsical touch.*

## 1
### Supplies

**Latex Wall Paint and Medium:**
  Taupe, satin sheen
  Ivory, semi-gloss sheen
  Neutral Glazing medium
  Pearl metallic acrylic craft paint

**Tools and Equipment:**
  Plumb line
  Ruler
  Pencil
  Sea sponge or sea sponging mitt
  Low tack masking tape

## 2
### Preparation

1. Prepare walls.
2. Paint walls with taupe paint. Allow to dry thoroughly.
3. At top of wall, make a pencil mark every 24" around room. In this room, I adjusted the width of stripes slightly to be sure a stripe was placed to wrap each corner. It's best not to have a stripe end at a corner because corners usually are not straight and the stripe will look wavy.
4. Drop a plumb line at each mark **(photo 1)** and run masking tape down wall in straight, vertical lines. Be sure tape is outside each vertical line **(photo 2)**.

## 3
### Sponging Stripes

1. Mix 1 part linen white paint and 3 parts glazing medium. Pour some of this glaze mixture in a paint tray.
2. Dampen sponge and squeeze or towel dry. Dip sponge in glaze mixture. Pounce sponge on paint tray to remove excess glaze mixture.
3. Working inside the 24" taped off areas, pounce loaded sponge onto wall so that you get a sharp, textured image **(photo 3)**. Do not rub or drag the sponge. Continue until all stripes have been sponged. Remove tape before paint dries. Let paint dry overnight.

## 4
### Metallic Dots

Pour some pearl metallic paint on a disposable plate. Dip the end of your index finger in paint, blot your finger on a clean area of the tray, and print dots on the taupe (unsponged) stripes **(photo 4)**. (These prints are 9-10" apart.) *You may wish to practice your technique on a piece of paper before finger printing on the wall.* 🍂

# HERE'S HOW

### 1

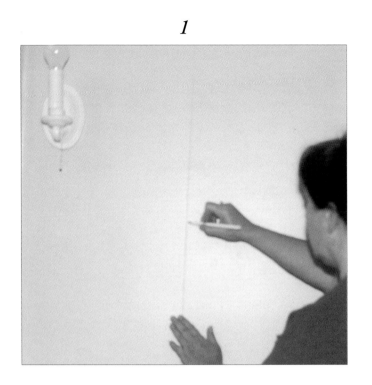

### 2

### 3

### 4

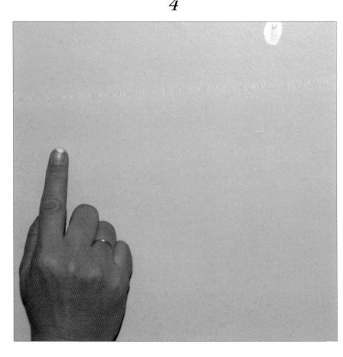

# BRUSHED TEXTURES

*Brush texturing is just that—using a bristle brush to stroke a colored glaze to create texture over a painted basecoat.Brushes of varying sizes and stiffness can add subtle or dramatic textured effects to a wall. It is fun to experiment with a variety of brushes and techniques to create an effect you like.*

*The inspiration for the colors in this room came from the Provence-influenced sofa fabric, which has a deep ultramarine blue background with lime green, sage, and gold accents. The springtime view from the wall of windows in this second-story retreat is of lush, green foliage, and the owners chose to bring that spring green color inside all year long. To add a textural interest to the walls, sage green glaze was brushed over lime green painted walls, using cross-hatched, overlapping strokes.*

*The wooden window trim was painted white. Because of the wonderful view, the windows were emphasized with a dark blue border that was stenciled with a fish and wave motif.*

## SUPPLIES

Many different types of **bristle brushes** can be used to create textures and patterns. Stiffer bristles create more pronounced textures; softer bristles provide a more muted effect. The colored glaze mixture is made by stirring **paint glaze, acrylic craft paint, latex wall paint, or stencil paint** into a **neutral glazing medium**.

### Supplies Pictured for Brushed Textures:

1.  Glazing medium, neutral
2.  Colored paint glaze, option for mixing with glazing medium
3.  Acrylic craft paint, option for mixing with glazing medium
4.  Latex wall paint, option for mixing with glazing medium
5.  Stir stick
6.  Wide, soft bristle brush (also called a "fabric weaver"), option for creating texture on surface
7.  Stencil brush, option for creating texture on surface
8.  French brush, option for creating texture on surface
9.  Stippler brush, option for creating texture on surface
10. Wall paint brush, option for creating texture on surface

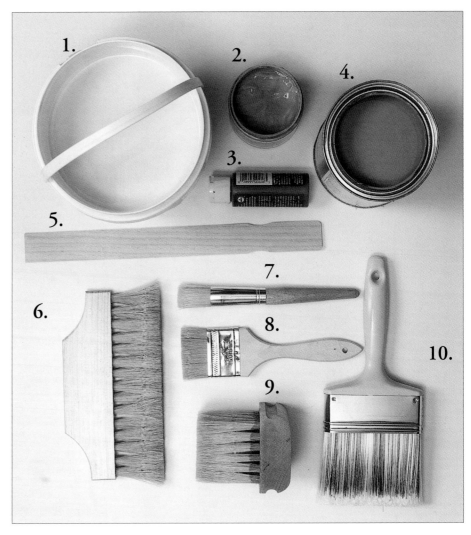

*(Photo on page 55)*

* *Instructions for the Spattered Trunk can be found in the "Spattering" section.*

* *See "Stenciling" section for stenciling information on window border.*

## HERE'S HOW

### 1

Mix glazing medium and paint. A 50/50 mix would be a good starting point. Mix small amounts first and experiment with the effect before mixing an entire batch for the room.

### 2

Pour some of the glaze mixture on a disposable plate. Load brush, using plate as a palette.

### 3

Brush glaze mixture on prepared surface, using bristles of brush to create texture and pattern.

## SAMPLES OF BRUSHED TEXTURES

*Linen texture stroked horizontally and vertically with fabric weaver brush*

*Overlapping swirls created with wall paint brush*

# FAMILY ROOM WALLS

## 1
## *Supplies*

**Latex Wall Paint and Medium:**

Lime green, satin finish　　Sage green, satin finish
Glazing medium, neutral　　Ultramarine blue, satin finish

**Tools & Equipment:**

2" brush with stiff, short bristles, such as a stippler brush or a
　French brush
Paint brushes and rollers
Low tack masking tape
Plumb line, Bubble level, Pencil, Ruler

## 2
## *Preparation*

1. Prepare walls.
2. Paint walls with two coats lime green paint. Allow to dry between coats. Let last coat dry overnight.
3. Mix equal amounts sage green paint and glazing medium. Test this mixture by brushing some on an inconspicuous portion of wall. Wipe off glaze mixture immediately with a damp cloth if you're not happy with the result. Experiment with varying amounts of glazing medium and paint until you have a result that pleases you.

## 3
## *Brush Textured Walls*

1. Mask off two opposite walls, using masking tape in the corners **(photo below)**. (This makes it easier to create texture in the corners without overlapping the strokes on the adjacent wall.)
2. Brush glaze mixture on two walls, using cross-hatch strokes. You want distinct strokes to show, so don't overbrush. Simply brush once and move on to next brush stroke. Continue until both walls have been brush stroked. Remove tape. Allow to dry completely.
3. Tape off at corners of remaining two walls to protect walls already completed. Brush glaze mixture on remaining walls, following same procedure. Remove tape. Allow to dry. ✃

### CREATING A WINDOW BORDER

1. To measure for the window border, make marks every 5-6" that are 5-1/2" away from window trim. Use a ruler and a pencil to connect the marks so that you have drawn a border around window. Use a plumb line and a bubble level to check the horizontal and vertical straightness of the lines. (Windows aren't always perfectly level, but if your border isn't level, you'll notice.)
2. With masking tape, tape outside of marked lines.
3. Paint window border with ultramarine blue. Only one coat was used, allowing some of the green wall to show through in places to give a more casual, worn look. Remove tape. Allow to dry completely. ✃

*See "Stenciling" section for information on stenciling borders.*

# COMBING & WOOD GRAINING

*To create combed and wood grained designs, a colored glaze is applied over a basecoated surface and partially removed by pulling a combing tool over the surface. Wonderful effects can be achieved. The process is simple and fun.*

## SUPPLIES

Tools such as **rubber combs, a pencil eraser, or a graining tool** can be used to pull across the glazed surface to create combed effects. The glaze that remains on the surface creates the design. Different types of combs produce different patterns and effects. Handheld rubber combs work well on furniture and in small areas. Wall combs, attached to a handle, cover large areas easily. The colored glaze mixture is made by tinting **neutral glazing medium** with **colored paint glaze, acrylic craft paint, or latex wall paint.**

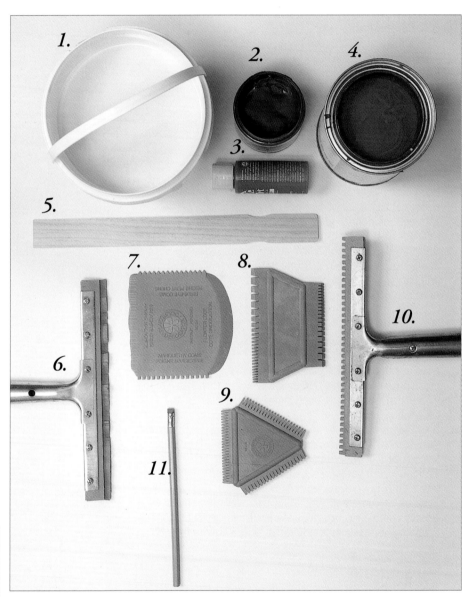

**Wood Graining Tool**

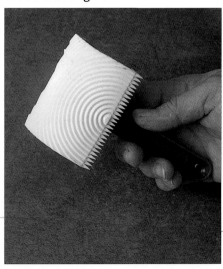

### Supplies Pictured for Combing and Wood Graining:

1. Glazing medium, neutral
2. Colored paint glaze, option for mixing with glazing medium
3. Acrylic craft paint, option for mixing with glazing medium
4. Latex wall paint, option for mixing with glazing medium
5. Stir stick
6. Wall comb option
7, 8, 9. Rubber combs, options for walls or furniture
10. Wall comb
11. Pencil eraser, for making wood grain

# HERE'S HOW

### 1

### 2

Fill any dents or cracks in the surface and sand smooth. Wipe away dust. Basecoat surface. Allow to dry. Mix glazing medium with paint **(photo 1)**.

Work on one section at a time, using masking tape to separate sections. You want to create the look of different pieces of wood joined together—the way a real wooden door looks. Using a stippler brush, pounce glaze mixture on the painted surface **(photo 2)**.

### 3

### 4

Pull a rubber comb through the glaze, using a wavy motion on some areas and a straight motion on other areas **(photo 3)**.

Lightly pull the fabric weaver brush across the combed surface to blend the color slightly. You don't want to remove the combing lines, just soften them **(photo 4)**. This softening step can also be used after the next two steps.

### 5

### 6

Create a more pronounced grain in some areas by pulling a pencil eraser that's been cut in a wedge shape over the combed glaze **(photo 5)**.

Another way to create the look of wood grain is with the tool shown on page 58 made especially for this purpose. Basecoat surface. Allow to dry. Mix glazing medium with paint. Using a stippler brush, pounce glaze mixture on the painted surface. Rock and drag the graining tool across glazed surface **(photo 6)**.

# WOOD GRAINED FARMHOUSE DOOR

*An unsightly, battered door was given new life and beauty with glazing medium and a variety of tools that, together, were used to create a combed wood grain finish. A polished doorknob and plate complete the transformation.*

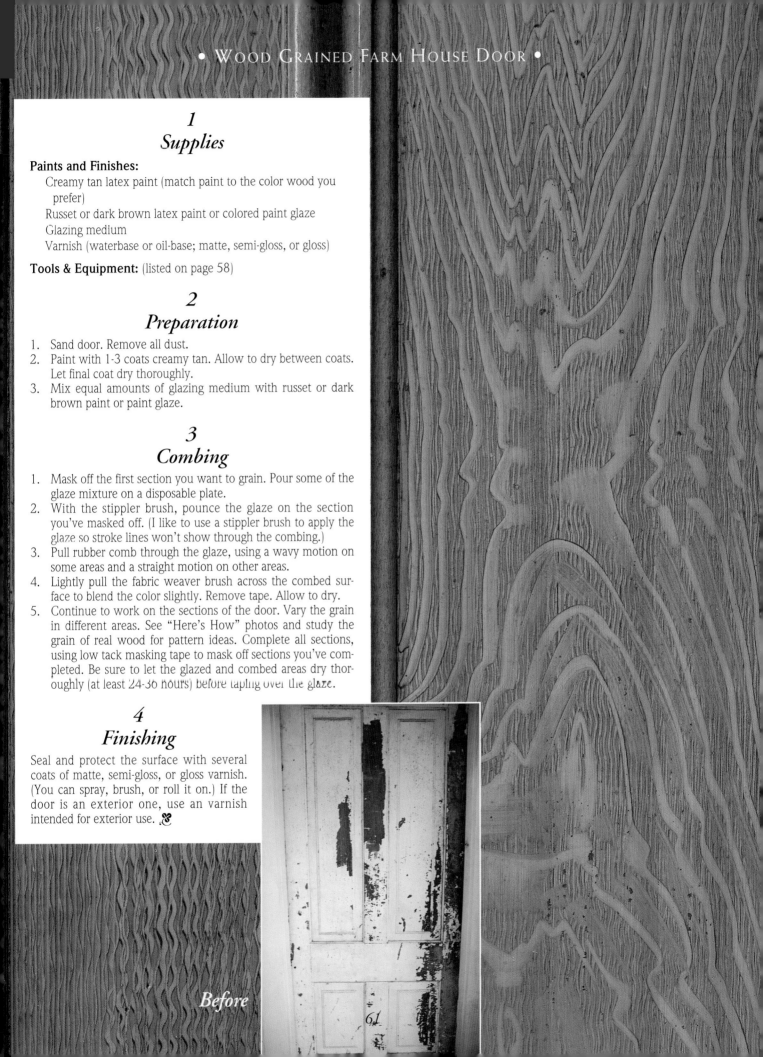

# 1
## Supplies

**Paints and Finishes:**

Creamy tan latex paint (match paint to the color wood you prefer)

Russet or dark brown latex paint or colored paint glaze

Glazing medium

Varnish (waterbase or oil-base; matte, semi-gloss, or gloss)

**Tools & Equipment:** (listed on page 58)

# 2
## Preparation

1. Sand door. Remove all dust.
2. Paint with 1-3 coats creamy tan. Allow to dry between coats. Let final coat dry thoroughly.
3. Mix equal amounts of glazing medium with russet or dark brown paint or paint glaze.

# 3
## Combing

1. Mask off the first section you want to grain. Pour some of the glaze mixture on a disposable plate.
2. With the stippler brush, pounce the glaze on the section you've masked off. (I like to use a stippler brush to apply the glaze so stroke lines won't show through the combing.)
3. Pull rubber comb through the glaze, using a wavy motion on some areas and a straight motion on other areas.
4. Lightly pull the fabric weaver brush across the combed surface to blend the color slightly. Remove tape. Allow to dry.
5. Continue to work on the sections of the door. Vary the grain in different areas. See "Here's How" photos and study the grain of real wood for pattern ideas. Complete all sections, using low tack masking tape to mask off sections you've completed. Be sure to let the glazed and combed areas dry thoroughly (at least 24-36 hours) before taping over the glaze.

# 4
## Finishing

Seal and protect the surface with several coats of matte, semi-gloss, or gloss varnish. (You can spray, brush, or roll it on.) If the door is an exterior one, use an varnish intended for exterior use. ❈

*Before*

61

# EXAMPLES OF TEXTURES USING A VARIETY OF TOOLS

**Combed Stripes**
*Honey colored glaze was applied over a white background, then combed with a wall comb.*

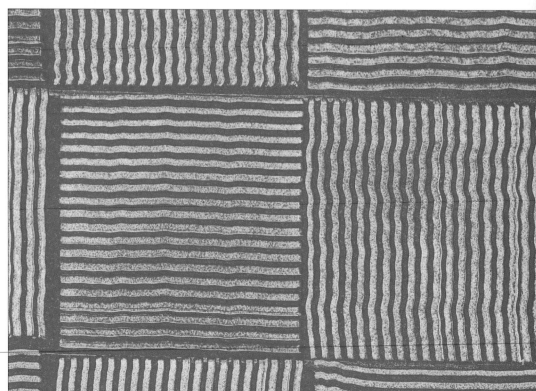

**Combed Checks**
*Deep rose glaze was applied over a white background, then combed with rubber comb. The width of the comb determined the size of the squares; changing directions created the checkerboard.*

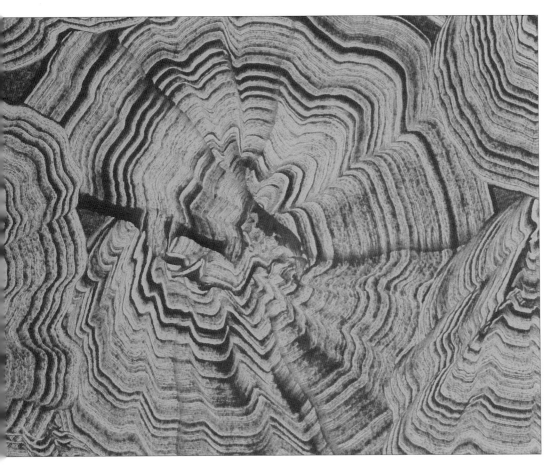

**Combed Waves**
*Dark green glaze was applied over a medium green background, then combed with the malachite edge of a multi-purpose comb.*

**Combed Graduated Stripes**
*Deep blue glaze was applied over a pale blue background, then combed with a graduated comb.*

# DISTRESSING

*A distressed finish imitates the wear and tear of use on wood surfaces. The surface is painted, and then the paint is removed in areas that would naturally become worn over time. It's a terrific way to finish an interesting old piece of furniture that's not a fine antique, like this cabinet with turned legs. Paint colors for the piece were chosen to coordinate with the room's decor.*

*A distressed finish can also give the look of age to a new piece of furniture.*

## SUPPLIES

Two or more colors of **latex paint** are layered for a distressed finish. After painting the first layer of paint, **wax or paraffin** is rubbed on the surface. After painting the second layer, medium and coarse **sandpaper** and a **metal scraper** are used to remove paint from the surface. (You can also use an **electric hand sander** to remove paint.) In the areas where wax has been applied, the paint is easier to sand and scrape off, creating the distressed look.

### Supplies Pictured for Creating a Distressed Finish:

*1, 2. Latex wall paint*
*3, 4. Medium (#220) and coarse (#100) sandpaper*
*5. Wax stick, to apply to surface to make paint easier to sand off*
*6. Metal scraper, for distressing wood and scraping paint*
*7. Foam brush, for applying basecoat of paint*
*Optional: Electric sander*

## DISTRESSED CABINET

*Pictured on page 65*

Prepare wood piece according to general instructions. The first paint color used to basecoat cabinet is green flat latex paint. Paraffin wax is rubbed on spots on this dry painted finish. White satin sheen latex paint is then applied to entire cabinet (two coats may be needed for total coverage). After drying, a scraper is used to scrape off paint. Then 100 grit sandpaper is used to remove some of the white paint layer. The sanding is finished with 220 grit sandpaper. An electric sander can be used on larger areas, but you'll need to hand sand in tight areas and crevices. Pay special attention to creating a worn look on the edges. Wipe away dust. ❧

# ANTIQUING WITH GLAZE

*With use and over time, paint can develop an attractive patina. It's possible to create the look of age by applying colored glaze on a painted surface. On this wooden table, areas were painted with different bright colors and a black glaze mixture was used as an antiquing medium to make the colors appear mellow and blended.*

## SUPPLIES

You can create an antiquing medium by mixing **glazing medium** with **colored paint glaze, latex paint, or acrylic craft paint.** Rub the glaze mixture on the surface with a moist **cellulose sponge.** In tight areas, apply with a **small paint brush.** You can also use **pre-mixed brush-on antiquing or an antiquing spray.** To apply, follow manufacturer's instructions.

### Supplies Pictured for Antiquing

1. Glazing medium
2. Colored paint glaze, for mixing with glazing medium
3. Acrylic craft paint, for mixing with glazing medium
4. Pre-mixed brush-on antiquing or stain as an option
5. Pre-mixed antiquing spray as an option
6. Stir stick
7. Small paint brush, for brushing antiquing glaze into crevices or corners
8. Cellulose sponge, for applying antiquing to surface

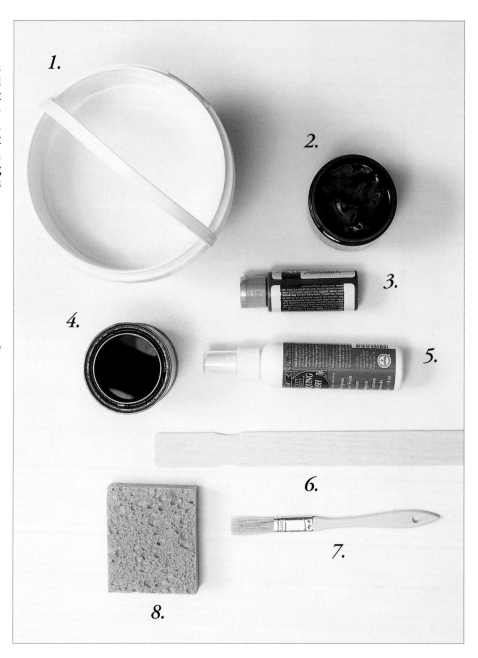

*See step-by-step instructions for Multi-colored Table on page 68.*

# MULTI-COLORED TABLE INSTRUCTIONS

## 1
## Supplies

- **Surface:** Wooden table with two drawers
- **Paints & Finishes:**
    Black latex paint, paint glaze, or gel
      paint
    Acrylic craft paint: Navy blue, Maroon,
      Yellow, Off white
    Glazing medium

- **Tools & Equipment:**
    Cellulose sponge
    Foam brushes
    Masking tape
    Bristle brush
    Container for mixing antiquing
    Sandpaper, 220 grit

## 2
## Preparation

1. Remove drawers and drawer pulls. Sand the surface smooth. Wipe away dust.

2. Decide on a color scheme for your table, using colorways as a guide. Paint each area with 1-2 coats of the color you have chosen. Use masking tape to section off the areas or paint carefully with a trim brush. Allow to dry.

## 3
## Antiquing

1. Mix equal amounts of glazing medium and black paint. Moisten a cellulose sponge and squeeze out excess water.
2. Rub entire piece with the glaze mixture. Make the antiquing as intense or subtle as you prefer. Allow to dry.

## 4
## Finishing

1. Seal the surfaces with matte sealer. Allow to dry.
2. Replace drawer pulls and drawers. 🐝

## COLORWAYS

**Basecoat:**
  *Camel*
**Antiquing:**
  *Dark brown*

**Basecoat:**
*Mint green*
**Antiquing:**
*Dark green*

**Basecoat:**
*White*
**Antiquing:**
*Burgundy*

**Basecoat:**
*Pale blue*
**Antiquing:**
*Dark blue*

# CRACKLING

*The age and character that naturally takes years of wind and weather to achieve can be easily created on painted surfaces with crackle medium. On the two cabinets shown in this chapter, two paint colors have been sandwiched around a coat of crackle medium to create the distinctive finish. When the second color was applied, cracks formed that revealed the first color.*

## SUPPLIES

A crackled finish is achieved by using **crackle medium,** which is a clear, easy to apply liquid. Crackle medium does not crack, but any water-based medium that is applied on top of the dried crackle medium reacts with it by shrinking and cracking, creating the distinctive crackled look.

There are two ways to create crackled finishes. One-color crackle uses **latex paint** as a basecoat. Crackle medium is applied, then a **clear waterbase varnish** becomes the top coat. The crackle medium causes the varnish to form cracks. When dry, the cracks are rubbed with an antiquing medium, leaving color in the cracks.

Two different paint colors are used for two-color crackle—one for the basecoat and another for the topcoat, with the crackle medium applied between the two coats.

### Supplies Pictured for Crackling:

*1, 2. Latex wall paint, for painting surface*
*3.  Crackle medium*
*4.  Brush-on clear varnish, for the topcoat in the one-color crackle process*
*5.  Foam brush for applying paint, crackle medium, and varnish*

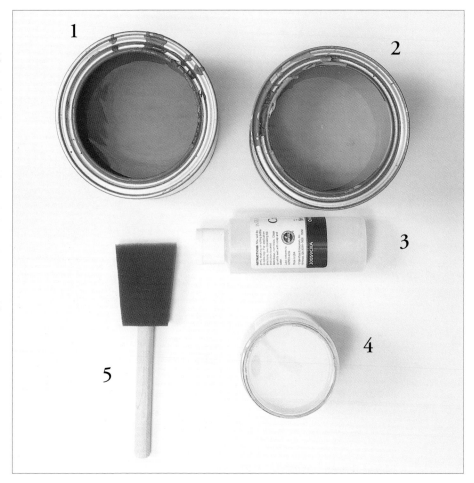

## CRACKLING TIPS

- A thicker topcoat of paint or varnish will create large cracks; a thin coat will create smaller cracks.
- Be sure to apply the topcoat using long, smooth strokes. You can't go back later and smooth it out.
- When you apply your topcoat, load the brush with enough paint to complete the stroke. .
- Don't overwork or overstroke the topcoat—that can make the cracks disappear.
- The more you practice, the better your results will be. Try your paint colors and technique on pieces of scrap lumber or poster board before working on your furniture piece.
- When working on a crackled piece, work horizontally when applying the topcoat so the crackling won't sag or drag. (This is especially important when trying to produce large cracks, which require a thick topcoat.) To prevent sagging, apply the topcoat to one side of the piece at a time and let it dry. Then turn the piece and work another side and let it dry, and so on. You can also remove drawers and doors and lay them flat to topcoat.
- Another crackling method, called "crusting" is achieved by dragging a brush over the crackled surface while the topcoat is still wet. This achieves a damaged crackle effect. ⅋

This chest of drawers top was done using the two color crackle method. White latex paint was used for the basecoat layer and red latex paint used for the topcoat. See the following pages for step-by-step instructions. ℰ

# HERE'S HOW — ONE COLOR TECHNIQUE

### *1*

Basecoat surface with 1-3 coats of paint for an even coverage. Allow to dry thoroughly. Brush crackle medium on painted surface. Allow to dry. When dry, the surface should look uniformly shiny. If it doesn't look uniformly shiny, apply a second coat. Allow the second coat to dry according to manufacturer's instructions.

### *2*

Use a clean, dry brush to apply a coat of waterbase varnish over the crackle medium, working quickly, one area at a time. Smooth out the varnish as you work each long stroke. Cracks will form instantly. Allow to dry. *If using the two-color method, you would apply your second paint color now instead of clear varnish. Cracks would appear instantly.*

### *3*

Rub antiquing medium into cracks with a cellulose sponge. Allow to dry. Use a pre-mixed antiquing medium or make your own by mixing acrylic craft paint with neutral glazing medium. *If using the two-color paint method, this step is not needed.*

## TWO COLOR TECHNIQUE

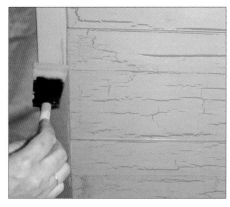

In the two color technique, the first color is applied as the basecoat. When thoroughly dry, brush on the crackle medium and allow to dry until uniformly shiny. With a clean dry brush, apply the second color, which crackles as it dries, revealing the first color in the cracks.

The cabinet shown on page 73 was created with the two-color crackle method. The basecoat layer of paint was teal green. Mustard was used for the topcoat.

***Example of Two Color Crackle:***
*Basecoat: Camel*
*Topcoat: White*

***Example of One Color Crackle:***
*Basecoat: Blue*
*Topcoat: Waterbase varnish*
*Antiquing: Dark blue*

# SPATTERING

*This wooden trunk on legs makes a perfect coffee table. It was painted with two colors that coordinate with fabrics chosen for the room. The rounded shapes on the top and sides were created by making a taped "stencil" with masking tape and a pencil compass. Spattering was done with both paint colors to unify the design and add texture.*

## SUPPLIES

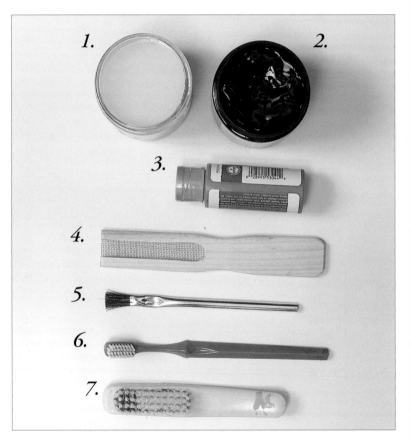

For spattering, **colored paint glaze or acrylic craft paint** is mixed in equal amounts with **glazing medium** to provide the proper ink-like consistency to the paint. Spatters can be created on a surface with a **spatter tool**, which is a mesh screen on a handle (you use a brush to rub paint through the screen), or with a **toothbrush** or a **nail brush.**

### Supplies Pictured for Spattering:

1. *Glazing medium for mixing with paint to create ink like consistency to paint*
2. *Colored paint glaze, as an option for mixing with glazing medium*
3. *Acrylic craft paint, as an option for mixing with glazing medium*
4, 5. *Spatter tool, option for spattering*
6. *Toothbrush, option for spattering*
7. *Nail brush, option for spattering*

## HERE'S HOW

### *Using a Spattering Tool*

Hold spattering tool over surface. Dip tips of brush bristles in paint. Rub brush tips over mesh screen of spattering tool. Drops of paint will spatter on surface.

### *Using a Toothbrush*

Dip bristles of toothbrush in paint. Hold brush over surface. Run your thumb over the bristles to release paint and spatter surface.

# AGED PLASTER

*Shown in this chapter are two ways to create the aged plaster look. One way, shown on the walls of a French cafe, is a faux finishing technique. The cafe's owners wanted a time-worn, old world look in their newly renovated storefront space.*

*In the bathroom of a 1920s house, an appreciation for lovingly worn surroundings was the inspiration for finishing the plaster walls. Here, the look was created not with a faux finishing technique, but by applying a washed finish that enhances what had naturally occurred with age. The colors uncovered in the finishing were incorporated in a stamped border that mimics mosaic tiles.*

## SUPPLIES

The faux aged plaster technique requires many steps, but they are easy and the results are amazing. First, **pre-mixed plaster** is smoothed on the prepared wall and allowed to dry. The plaster is sealed. Then, on various areas of the wall, **paraffin or wax** is rubbed on the wall. Where this is done, the layers of paint to be applied will more easily sand off. One, two, or several layers of paint are then painted on wall, allowing each to dry thoroughly. Then the fun begins. Use a **hammer, scraper, or chisel** to gouge and dent the wall to the extent you desire. Using **coarse and medium sandpaper**, sand through layers of paint. (An **electric hand sander** is good for this.) When working with plaster, **always** wear a dust mask or use a respirator to protect your nose and mouth as you work. Be sure to keep the area well ventilated.

When you are satisfied with the appearance, glaze with a wash of color to finish and unify.

### Supplies Pictured for Aged Plaster:

1. *Pre-mixed plaster*
2. *Spreader for plaster*
3. *Scraper for scraping top layers of paint from surface*
4. *Paraffin for applying to first layer of paint*
5. *Sandpaper, medium (#150-200) and coarse (#100)*
6. *Hand sander*
7. *Dust mask .*

*The photo at right shows a closeup of the walls in the "Aged Plaster Bathroom." See page 78 for step-by-step instructions.*

# Aged Plaster Bathroom

*Old can be beautiful—or so think the owners of this 1920s bathroom. Faced with peeling paint and cracked plaster, they chose not to replace or restore the walls. Instead, what was happening naturally was enhanced with sanding, scraping, and a color wash.*

*The technique was a treasure hunt for colors. First a scraper was used to remove peeling paint. Next, with a hand sander, layers of color were uncovered and the surface was smoothed. When the desired look had been achieved, the walls were washed with an ivory glaze to mellow and blend the colors in all the layers.*

*The top layer of existing paint was off-white. This would be the predominant color influence. Under that was turquoise, followed by a bright green. Somewhere was a layer of gold, then came khaki. In some places the ivory colored plaster shows, in others the bare, cement-colored plaster undercoat can be seen. Before the final choice was made for the wash, several colors were tested on the walls. Because acrylic paint colors were mixed with a waterbase glazing medium, they could all be tried. Any color that didn't work could be wiped off with a damp rag. A gold wash, a khaki wash, a mushroom colored wash, and a darker green glaze all got wiped off. The ivory wash was chosen.*

*The color scheme for the room was chosen from the colors of the old layers of paint. Turquoise, green, and gold were chosen for the stamped mosaic trim and accessories such as towels. If the colors the owners uncovered hadn't been pleasing, a colored glaze could have been used to mask or alter the existing colors.*

## 1
## Supplies

- **Latex Paints & Mediums:**
  Ivory, satin sheen latex paint
  Warm gold, semi-gloss sheen latex paint
  White, semi-gloss sheen latex paint
  Glazing medium
- **Acrylic Craft Paint:** (for mosaic design)
  Ultramarine blue        Sage green
  Turquoise        Warm gold
- **Tools & Equipment;**
  Paint scraper
  Electric hand sander
  Sandpaper, 60 grit and 100 grit
  Cellulose sponge, sponging mitt, or
    mopping mitt
  Cellulose household sponge for creating
    mosaic design
  Scissors or craft knife
  Disposable plates
  Disposable cups
  Dust mask or respirator

## 2
## Preparation

1. Using a paint scraper, remove all peeling paint **(photo 1)**.
2. Using an electric sander and coarse sandpaper, begin removing layers of paint **(photo 2)**. Please wear a dust mask or respirator and keep the area well-ventilated.
3. Use medium sandpaper for the final sanding to smooth the wall surfaces.

## 3
## Glazing

1. Mix equal amounts of ivory paint and glazing medium in a paper cup to create a wash for the walls. Test the mixture. If it seems too opaque, add more glazing medium. When you achieve a proportion you like, use those proportions to mix about 1 quart of glaze.
2. Pour some of the mixture on a disposable plate. Moisten a cellulose sponge, sponging mitt, or mopping mitt with water. Squeeze out excess water. Dip sponge in glaze. Blot sponge on a clean plate to remove excess.
3. Using the sponge or mop, rub and dab wash on the wall **photo 3.** Continue until all walls have been washed with glaze mixture. Allow to dry.

## 4
## Stamping the Mosaic Design

1. Using a craft knife or scissors, cut a 3/4" square for each "tile" color from a dry cellulose sponge. (Four colors were used in this bathroom.)
2. Dampen sponge squares with water and squeeze out excess moisture.
3. In separate disposable cups, mix each acrylic craft color with glazing medium, using 2 parts paint and 1 part glazing medium.
4. Using a disposable plate as a palette, place a little of each color paint onto plate. Dip a sponge square into a color, then dab the sponge square on an empty plate to remove excess paint, and stamp the square on the wall. The top of the ceramic tile on the wall created the placement for the first row of stamping. The other two rows were placed above the first. We did not want the rows to be perfectly straight, so no measuring was needed.
5. Repeat stamping for each color. Here, the colors were stamped randomly.

## 5
## Finishing

1. Paint door, door trim, and window sashes with white paint.
2. Paint window trim with warm gold paint. 

*\* Dots and Dashes Towel Stand in photo at right instructions can be found in the "Stenciling Designs" section.*

## HERE'S HOW

**1**

**2**

**3**

# AGED PLASTER FRENCH CAFE

## 1
## Supplies

• **Paints & Coatings:**
Pre-mixed plaster
Plaster sealant
Yellow, satin finish latex paint
Ochre satin finish latex paint
Deep red, satin finish latex paint
Gold stencil paint
Glazing medium

• **Tools & Equipment Needed:**
Wax stick
Scraper
Hammer
Chisel
Sandpaper, 100 grit and 150 grit
Foam brush and/or bristle brush
Paint tray
Sponging mitt or sponge
Stencils for classical motifs
Stencil brush
Dust mask or respirator
Vacuum cleaner
*Optional:* Electric hand sander

*Newly decorated, Cafe Alsace in Decatur, Georgia looks as if it has been operating on the streets of a European city for generations. The deep ocher and red color scheme adds to the cozy feeling, and touches of gold remind us of Old World elegance. Above the wainscotting, the walls were given the faux aged plaster technique. The wainscotting was painted dark red and stenciled in gold with classical motifs.*

## 2
## Plastering and Waxing

1. Smooth pre-mixed plaster over the upper walls. Allow to dry.
2. Rub the upper walls randomly with wax. In places where wax has been applied, the paint will be easier to remove.

## 3
## Painting

Paint upper walls with 1-2 coats yellow paint. Let dry between coats. Let final coat dry.

## 4
## Distressing

1. Using a hammer and a chisel, gouge and dent the wall to create an aged, worn appearance.
2. With a paint scraper, scrape away some of the paint. In areas where wax was applied, the paint will scrape away easily.
3. Sand with coarse and medium sandpaper.
4. Vacuum walls to remove dust.

## 5
## Glazing

1. Mix 3 parts glazing medium with one part ochre paint. Dampen a sponging mitt or sponge. Use the mitt or sponge to rub the colored glaze over the surface. You can apply the glaze evenly or leave some areas unglazed—it's your choice. Let dry.

## 6
## Finishing

1. Paint wainscotting with deep red paint. Let dry.
2. Stencil motifs with gold paint below upper edge of wainscotting. ❦

# STENCILING DESIGNS

*Stenciling is a time-honored, traditional technique of applying paint through openings in a material that is resistant to paint to create a design with repeated patterns.*

*Pre-cut stencils are readily available in a wide array of styles suitable for every decor. You can also cut your own stencil designs, using stencil blank material and a craft knife, or create designs for stenciling with masking tape.*

*In this room, golden fish swim along golden waves in a stenciled window border.*

**Stenciled Window Border:**
*See page 84 for step-by-step instructions.*

# FISH WINDOW BORDER

*The stenciled waves and fish echo the gold in the sofa fabric and are a pleasurable motif for the frequent inhabitant of this room who enjoys fly-fishing.*

*For instructions on painting the Walls and Window Border, see the "Brush Textures" section*

## 1
## Supplies

- **Paints:**
  Gold acrylic craft paint or stencil paint
  Ultramarine blue latex satin sheen wall paint
- **Tools & Equipment:**
  Paint brushes and rollers
  Low tack masking tape
  Pencil
  Ruler
  Plumb line
  Bubble level
  Stencil blank material
  Stencil brush
  Tracing paper and pencil
  A piece of thick glass with smoothed or taped edges, to use as a cutting surface when cutting the stencil
  Craft knife
  Permanent fine tip marker

## 2
## Window Border

1. To measure for the window border, make marks that are 5-1/2" away from window trim **(photo 1)**. Use a ruler and a pencil to connect the marks so that you have drawn a border around window. Use a plumb line and a bubble level to check the horizontal and vertical straightness of the lines **(photo 2)**. (Windows aren't always perfectly level, but if your border isn't level, you'll notice.)
2. With masking tape, tape outside of marked lines **(photo 3)**.
3. Paint window border with ultramarine blue. Only one coat was used, allowing some of the green wall to show through in places to give a more casual, worn look. Remove tape. Allow to dry completely.

## 3
## Making the Stencil

1. Place tracing paper over stencil pattern in this book. Trace pattern on tracing paper with pencil.
2. Measure your window and adjust the design to fit your window. Because we wanted the design at each corner to look the same, we worked from the corners in towards the center on the tops, bottom, and sides of each window, adjusting the placement of the fish to accommodate the size of the window. Notice that the waves do not meet in the center, and that the fish swim in one direction—clockwise—around the window.
3. Trace your adjusted stencil pattern on stencil blank material with a fine tip marker.
4. Place the stencil blank material on the glass. Using a craft knife, carefully cut out the design.

## 4
## Stenciling

1. Position stencil on painted border and tape in place.
2. Load stencil brush with paint. Blot brush on paper towels to remove excess paint. Apply paint through openings in stencil **(photo 4)**. Use very little paint on the brush to avoid having the paint run under the stencil and create smears and smudges.
3. Keep moving stencil and applying paint around border until completed. 🎀

*Pattern for Stenciled Window Border - enlarge @155% on copy machine for actual size.*

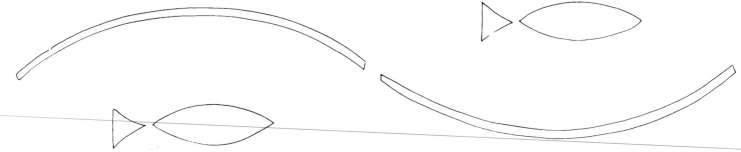

## HERE'S HOW

*1*

*2*

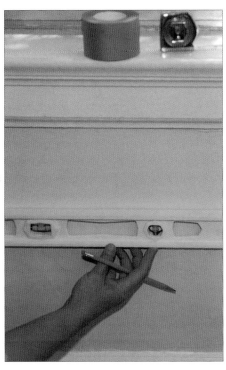

*3*

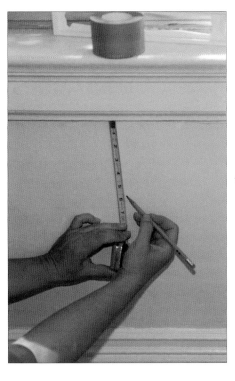

*4*

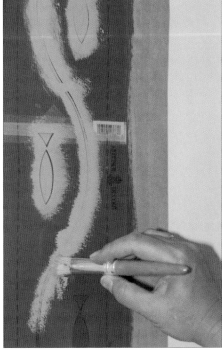

*CLOSEUP OF STENCILED
WINDOW BORDER*

# DOTS AND DASHES TOWEL STAND

*This old magazine table has been given a distressed and stenciled finish and a new life as a bathroom towel stand. Three neutral paint colors—tan, cream, and white—were layered, then distressed with a paint scraper and sanded so that all three layers are visible. (See chapter on "Aging and Antiquing" for more details about distressing.) Using a pre-cut stencil, squares and dashes were stenciled randomly with deep blue stencil gel paint.*

## 1
## Supplies

**Surface:** Wooden magazine table
**Paints and Finishes:**
   White latex paint, flat finish
   Cream latex paint, flat finish
   Tan latex paint, flat finish
   Deep blue stencil gel paint
   Matte sealer

**Tools & Equipment:**
   Pre-cut stencil, squares and dashes
     design
   Foam brush
   Bristle brush
   Small paint roller
   Sandpaper, 220 grit
   Paint scraper
   Paraffin or beeswax
   Stencil brush
   Paper towels

## 2
## Painting and Waxing

1. Sand surface. Wipe away dust.
2. Basecoat with tan paint. Allow to dry.
3. Apply wax randomly to the surface. In areas where the wax is applied, the paint will be easier to remove.
4. Paint table with cream paint. The waxed areas are resistant to paint. Keep stroking, and the paint will cover the wax. Allow to dry.
5. Apply wax randomly on the cream paint. (You don't have to wax the same areas.)
6. Paint with 1-2 coats white, making sure to achieve good coverage so the surface appears to be white. Allow to dry **no more than** 24 hours. The longer that it cures or dries, the harder it will be to scrape and to sand the surface.

## 3
## Distressing

1. Using the scraper, scrape and distress the surface. Where wax was applied, the scraper will remove paint. In some areas, the cream color will show; in other areas, the tan color will be visible.
2. Use sandpaper to remove any metal residue the scraper leaves on the painted surface. Wipe away dust.

## 4
## Stenciling

*The stencil designs were randomly placed.*
Position the stencil on the surface and pounce squares and dashes with deep blue stencil gel, using a stencil brush. Allow to dry.

## 5
## Finishing

1. Lightly sand the stenciled area to create an aged look to the stenciling that is appropriate with the distressed finish. Wipe away dust.
2. Seal with matte sealer. 🕸

# FALLING LEAVES DECK

*Natural leaves were the inspiration for this stenciled deck. A sponged and stenciled rectangular faux rug defines the deck's seating area. Over the rest of the deck, leaves were stenciled randomly. Real leaves from the owner's garden were used as patterns for cutting the stencils for the randomly placed leaves and for the fanciful "tassels" on the "rug." On the border of the "rug," real leaves were placed on the deck and the paint colors were sponged and pounced over the leaves.*

*This deck was painted before it was stenciled, but the design could also be stenciled on an unpainted deck. The rug can be any size you choose as long as it's appropriate for the size and shape of your deck. Use exterior floor paint for painting, stenciling, and sponging decks and porches. If the floor has been painted with an oil-base stain or paint, use an oil-base exterior paint for stenciling so the paint will adhere properly. If the floor is new wood or pressure treated wood that has cured, or if the floor has been stained or painted with an exterior waterbase product, use an exterior waterbase porch and floor paint to stencil and sponge. Don't put waterbase paint on top of oil-base paint or stain—it won't adhere as firmly and won't last as long.*

## 1
## Supplies

**Exterior Porch and Floor Paint:**
> Dark green
> Light green

**Tools & Equipment:**
> Leaves of assorted shapes and sizes,
>   (these are leaves from trees and shrubs)
> Craft knife
> Black fine tip permanent marker
> Stencil blank material
> Sponge or Sponging mitt
> French brush or stencil brush
> Masking tape
> Ruler and pencil
> Paint tray
> Chalk line
> Piece of glass with beveled or taped edges
>   or other hard surface for cutting stencil
> Artist's paint brush - #8 round or liner

## 2
## Preparation

1. Remove all dirt and moisture. *If the floor is new, pressure-treated lumber,* let it age at least one month before painting. Let paint cure one week before stenciling.
2. Measure and mark the outer edges of your "rug." (This one is 12-15" inside the outer edges of the deck.) Using a chalk line, connect the marks with a line of chalk. Stand back and study the lines to be sure they look straight and that the "rug" is an appropriate size.

## 3
## Cutting the Stencils

1. Arrange your collected leaves on a table or other firm surface. Place stencil blank material over leaves. Trace around edges of leaves with a permanent marker (**photo 1 on page 90**).
2. Place stencil blank material on glass cutting surface. Cut out leaf shapes with a craft knife (**photo 2 on page 90**).
3. Choose a long, narrow leaf to use as a pattern for the tassels. Cut a stencil for the tassels, using the long leaf shape.

## 4
## Stenciling the Random Leaves

1. Moisten the sponging mitt and blot on a towel to remove excess water. Position your stencil on the floor, using masking tape to hold it in place. Pour some light green paint in a paint tray.
2. Dip face of mitt in light green paint and lightly pounce paint through the opening in the stencil with the sponging mitt. Be sure the floor shows through the light green paint; you don't want solid coverage.
3. Continue to stencil leaves on the floor, scattering them randomly outside the outline of the "rug." Use a number of different sizes and shapes. Allow to dry. Rinse mitt.
4. On each leaf, replace the stencil and, with a French brush or a stencil brush, pounce dark green paint around the edges of the leaves and in the centers at times to create a randomly shaded appearance. Again, you don't want solid coverage. Do not completely cover over the light green or the floor. Allow to dry. Rinse mitt.

*Continued on page 90*

# FALLING LEAVES DECK

*continued from page 88*

## 5
### *Stenciling the "Rug"*

1. Measure and mark a border 10-15" wide on all four sides to create the border of the "rug."
2. Mask off the border, placing the tape to create squares on all four corners. Place a real leaf (I used large hydrangea leaves) in each corner **(photo 3)**.
3. Moisten the sponge or sponging mitt and blot on a towel to remove excess water. Dip face of mitt in light green paint and lightly pat over the leaf **(photo 4)**. Complete all four corners. Rinse mitt.
4. Pat the dark green color over the edges of each leaf to shade.
5. Remove the leaves. Lightly pounce the corners with light green to texture within the leaf shape.
6. With an artist's brush, paint veins in the leaves.
7. Lightly sponge the rest of the border with light green paint, using the sponging mitt. Allow to dry. Rinse mitt.
8. Position fresh leaves (I used leaves on stems that resemble the shapes of fern fronds) randomly on the border as though they had just fallen on the floor. Cut plenty of leaves so you'll have enough to create the entire border without re-using leaves.
9. With the sponge or sponging mitt, lightly pounce dark green color on the border and over the leaves. Rinse mitt.
10. Add more definition to the shapes by using the French brush or a stencil brush to pounce color along the edges of the leaf shapes. Use photo as a guide. Don't make these edges as dark as the corner areas. Remove the leaves immediately after pouncing. (If you wait to remove them until all four sides are completed, they might stick to the floor.) Repeat to complete the border. Allow to dry. Remove tape.
11. Using the sponge or sponging mitt, pounce the central area of the "rug" with light green. Sponge more heavily on the edges and in corners to shade.
12. Position the tassel stencil on one end of the "rug" and stencil the shapes with light green, using the sponging mitt. Allow to dry.
13. Reposition the stencil and stencil with dark green, using the French brush **(photo 5)**.
14. To create dimension and depth, mask off thin stripes on both sides of the border. Pounce with dark green, using the French brush. Remove tape. Allow to dry.

## 6
### *Finishing*

A sealer is not necessary. (I don't recommend applying a sealer on a floor that is exposed to rain, high humidity, or intense sunlight.) 🐝

*Closeup of leaf design*

### 1
### 2

3             4             5

# BLUE LEAVES CORNER CUPBOARD

*This blue and white stenciled corner cupboard would be at home in just about any room of the house. Use it in a kitchen for food storage and flatware, in a dining room to hold dishes and table linens, or in a family room or bedroom to display family photos and collections.*

*The wood is sanded and color stained with a white glaze mixture. Overlapping leaves cover the door panels and bands at the top and the bottom of the cabinet. Leaves also highlight the corners of the doors and the simple door and drawer pulls.*

## 1
## Supplies

**Surface:** Wooden corner cabinet
**Paints & Finishes:**
   White latex paint
   Delft blue latex paint
   Light blue latex paint
   Neutral Glazing medium
   Waterbase varnish or matte sealer

**Tools & Equipment:**
   Sponge brush
   2 stencil brushes
   Artist's liner brush
   Masking tape
   Sandpaper, 220 grit
   Stencil blank material
   Craft knife
   Fine tip permanent marker
   Piece of glass with beveled or taped
      edges or other hard surface for cutting
      stencil
   Pencil

## 2
## Preparation and Painting

1. Remove door and drawer pulls. Sand the surface smooth. Wipe away dust.
2. Mix equal amounts of neutral glazing medium and white paint. Use a sponge or brush to color stain the surface with the glaze mixture. Smooth out the color with a bristle brush, a rag, or a moist sponge. Allow to dry thoroughly.
3. Paint inside of the cabinet with delft blue. Paint bands of delft blue on trim areas, using photo as a guide for placement.

## 3
## Cutting the Stencil

1. Trace the leaf pattern on stencil blank material with a fine tip marker. You will need to make 4 stencils as shown on pattern.
2. Place the stencil blank material on the glass cutting surface. Carefully cut around the shapes with a craft knife.

## 4
## Stenciling

*Place the stenciling in areas that are appropriate for your furniture piece. I stenciled inside the door panels, along the top and bottom of the cabinet, at the corners of the doors, on the drawers, and on the pulls.*

1. Pour a teaspoon each of delft blue and light blue paint on a disposable plate. Don't mix the colors. Position the stencil.
2. Dip the stencil brush in light blue. Blot the brush on a paper towel. Using very little paint on the brush, lightly stroke paint on the leaf. Repeat, stenciling all overlays. Allow to dry.
3. Use the same overlays to shade the leaves. Position the stencil over the leaf shape and, using the second stencil brush, lightly stroke with delft blue. Use photo as a guide for the amount of shading needed.
4. Continue by repeating the stenciling of the four overlays until all areas you wish to stencil are complete. Allow to dry.
5. With the liner brush, add strokes to suggest veins in the leaves. Allow to dry.

## 5
## Finishing

1. Seal the surface with two to three coats waterbase varnish or matte sealer. Let dry between coats.
2. When final coat is dry, replace door and drawer pulls. ❦

***See page 94 for closeup view of design detail and cutting pattern.***

# BLUE LEAVES CORNER CUPBOARD
## Pattern for Leaf Stencil

Cut 4 stencils:

——————— (straight lines) = 1st overlay

· · · · · · · (dotted lines) = 2nd overlay

— — — — (broken lines) = 3rd overlay

⌐ ⌐ ⌐ ⌐ = 4th overlay

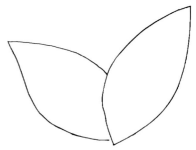

Position for corner leaves. Use a leaf from stencil #1 to create this design.

*(photo at right shows a closeup of the stencil design)*

# STAMPED DESIGNS

*Stamping is a quick, easy way to create a handpainted look on walls and furniture. Stamping can be done with pre-cut stamps or printing blocks, which are available in a wide variety of designs. You can also cut your own stamps from wood, vegetables, sponges, or dense foam stamp material. Found and natural objects, such as leaves, can be used as stamps to create stamped designs. Colored paint glaze, a translucent medium with a gel-like consistency, is ideal for stamping.*

***Her Private Garden:***
*See step-by-step instructions and photos on page 100.*

# STAMPED DESIGNS

## HERE'S HOW

### 1

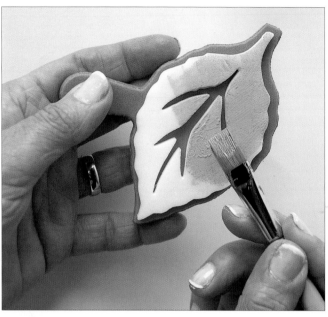

Load the stamp with glaze. A flat artist's brush works well to coat the stamp evenly. Brush the glaze to the edge of the design.

### 2

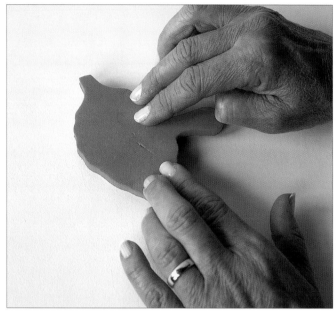

Hold the stamp by the handle and gently place it on the surface without sliding it. Press with fingertips to print.

### 3

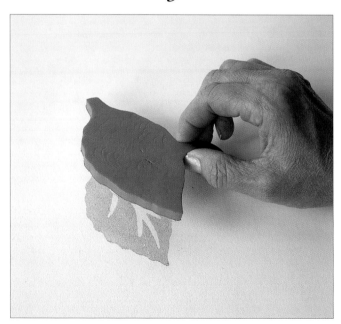

Use the handle to lift the stamp. Move to another section and repeat the process. You should be able to produce 2 or 3 prints before applying more glaze.

### *Completed design*

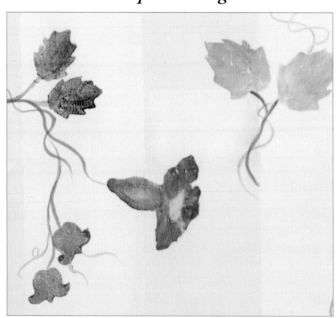

This photo shows a completed design. A liner brush is used to connect the flowers and leaves with vines and tendrils.
*The photo on page 99 shows a portion of the wall in "Her Private Garden". For detailed instructions, see page 100.

# HER PRIVATE GARDEN

*This fence and flowers wall border design is perfect for a little lady's room as shown here or a sunroom—it brings the outdoors in and adds a cheerful whimsy to any room. The picket fence is created with a cardboard template and masking tape, and the flowers and butterflies are stamped in bright, beautiful paint glaze colors that were chosen to coordinate with the colors in the bed coverings, draperies, and upholstery.*

## 1
### Supplies

**Latex Wall Paint:**
  White
  Pale gray
**Colored Paint Glaze:**
  Deep green
  Ivy green
  Pink
  Deep rose
  Yellow
  Dark blue
  Medium blue

**Tools & Equipment:**
  Morning glories foam stamp designs
  Small flowers foam stamp designs
  Butterflies foam stamp designs
  Level
  Ruler and colored pencil (choose a color slightly deeper than the wall color)
  Low tack masking tape
  Craft knife
  Poster board, 32" long for cutting picket fence template
  Small paint roller (2-3" wide)
  #12 flat artist brush
  Liner artist brush
  Disposable plates or paint trays
  Moist rag or cloth

## 2
### Preparation

Clean walls to remove any dust or grease. *If the walls are freshly painted,* allow the paint to cure according to manufacturer's instructions. Test the masking tape on an inconspicuous part of the wall to be sure the tape won't damage the paint or the wall when it's removed. Do not allow tape to stay on walls overnight.

## 3
### Measure, Mark, and Mask Off the Fence

*The size of the picket fence is determined by the size of the room. Here each picket is 32" tall and 3" wide. The pickets are positioned 2-1/2" apart so the space between the pickets is not as wide as the picket itself. The cross rails are 2" wide, which is—incidentally—the width of the level used for placing them.*

1. Cut a picket template from poster board. For tracing the picket, I used a colored pencil that's a slightly deeper shade of yellow than the wall—this allows me to see the outlines without making dark marks on the wall.
2. To begin tracing, find the center of the wall and mark the wall 30" above the top of the baseboard. (I started in the most visible part of the room so the fence would fit evenly and properly in between the windows.) Measure to the left and right of that first mark 1-1/2" for the first 3" wide picket. Measure and mark the walls for the pickets and spaces, marking 2-1/2", then 3" at the 30" height and at the baseboard. Use a level to make sure your lines are vertical. When you get close to a corner, you may have to adjust the spacing of the pickets, making them a little closer together or a little farther apart, so a picket won't end up in a corner.
3. Position the picket template at the marks and trace around the template **(photo 1 )**.
4. To mark the cross rails, measure up from the baseboard 3-4" for the lower rail and 28-29" for the upper rail. Using a level, mark the cross rails.
5. Working one area of the wall at a time, place low tack masking tape along the outlines of the pickets and cross rail. Press the tape firmly where it intersects. Tape only an area as large as you can paint immediately, because you do not want to leave the masking tape in place overnight—you want to tape, paint, and shade the pickets and remove the tape within hours. (That way, you can be sure you won't damage the wall.) Tape off the molding in the area where you've taped the pickets.

## 4
### Painting and Shading the Pickets

1. Use a small paint roller or brush to paint the pickets with white **(photo 2)**. It may take 2 coats. Allow to dry.
2. Dip a stencil brush in gray paint and blot on paper towels. Shade one side of each picket. To shade the cross rails and make them appear to recede, add tape vertically where the rails cross the pickets and shade the rails. Make sure you use a very dry brush; you want to create a pale, shadowy effect.
3. Remove the tape slowly, gently, and carefully. Repeat, taping and painting remaining areas of the wall, working one area at a time, until the picket fence is complete. Allow to dry and remove all tape.

## 5
### Stamping the Flowers, Leaves, and Butterflies

1. Stamp the flowers, leaves, and butterflies over and around the painted picket fence **(photo 3)**. Use the photographs as a guide for placement and colors. Follow these steps to stamp:
   * Squeeze a small amount of one of the paint glaze colors on a disposable plate.
   * With the flat brush, apply a thin coat of paint glaze to the stamp.
   * Position the stamp on the wall and, without sliding, press the stamp on the wall and lift.
2. Using a liner brush with slightly diluted green paint glaze, add tendrils, stems, and vines to connect the flowers and leaves. 🏵

### 1

### 2

### 3

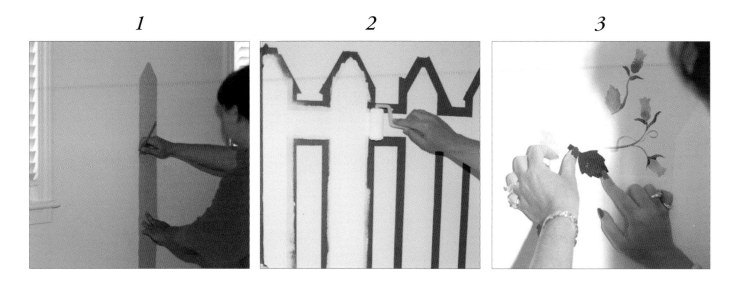

*Picket Fence Wall Border with Stamped Flowers*

# STREAMSIDE LEAVES BED TABLE

*Mother Nature has provided us with a bountiful resource for stamped design materials. Real leaves found in the backyard are used to stamp the design on this bedside table. The natural grain of the wood provides a perfect background for the leaf design and is in keeping with the effect of "bringing the outside in".*

## 1
## *Supplies*

**Surface:** Wooden table
**Paints & Finishes:**
  Medium green latex paint
  Green colored paint glaze
  Cream colored paint glaze
  Waterbase varnish

**Tools & Equipment:**
  Natural real leaves from the yard, trees
    or bushes (the softer and more pliable
    the leaf, the better—look for leaves
    that have a definite ridge along the
    vein line)
  Paper towels
  Sandpaper, 220 grit
  Small paint roller and/or foam brush
    and/or bristle brush
  Tack cloth or soft cloth
  Artist's paint brush - #12 flat
  Wax paper
  Foam brush
  Bristle brush

## 2
## *Preparation*

1. Sand table until smooth. Wipe away dust.
2. Use masking tape to mask off table apron and lower shelf. Paint apron and shelf with green paint. Allow to dry thoroughly. Lightly sand and remove all dust.
3. Paint with a second coat of green latex paint. Allow to dry.

## 3
## *Stamping Leaves*

*Before you stamp the leaf shapes on your table, make some test prints on a piece of poster board or scrap lumber. Experiment with the amount of paint glaze you apply—you want just enough for a crisp, clear print. If the glaze seeps out under the edge, you are using too much glaze. See step-by-step photos on page 104.*

1. Position leaves on the table, arranging them in a way that's pleasing to you.
2. Cover your work surface with wax paper. Pick up a leaf and, with the #12 brush, apply a coat of green paint glaze to the underside of the leaf and the stem **(photo 1)**. Position the leaf on the table surface **(photo 2)**, place a paper towel on top of it, and gently press the leaf area in the middle and along the edge. (Any excess paint glaze will be absorbed by the paper towel.)
3. Gently remove the paper towel **(photo 3)**. Using one finger to hold the leaf in place, lift the leaf off the surface from the stem end, being careful not to smear the design **(photo 4)**.
4. Choose another leaf and make another pressing, using the same technique.
5. After you've printed all the green leaves, print leaves on the green table apron and shelf with cream paint glaze. Allow to dry thoroughly.

## 4
## *Finishing*

Seal the surface with 2-3 coats waterbase varnish. Allow to dry thoroughly between coats. Lightly sand the surface before applying the final coat. 🐝

*For a closeup view of the table and step-by-step photos, see page 104 - 105.*

# STREAMSIDE LEAVES BED TABLE

## HERE'S HOW

### 1

### 2

### 3

### 4

## • PAINTING FROM PATTERNS •

# DESIGN PAINTING

*Painted designs are a way to create a coordinated, custom look and add color and interest to walls and furniture. A painted wall border, like the tulip border pictured here, brings the garden indoors all year long.*

*Painting the designs in this book is almost like painting by numbers. The patterns for each design are included; they can be enlarged or reduced as needed to fit your painting surface. Acrylic craft paints, used to paint the designs, come in a wide array of pre-mixed colors and are easy to use, even for beginners. Project photos provide guidance for colors and placement. Even if you've never painted before, you can create handpainted, beautiful designs.*

***Countryside Tulips Border:***
*See step-by-step instructions on page 110.*

106

# DESIGN PAINTING

*This wall border, painted just above the baseboard, reinforces the color scheme introduced by the upholstery and curtain fabrics. The pale yellow walls are a warm, neutral background for the colorful border.*

## SUPPLIES

Trace the design on **tracing paper** with a **pencil**. The pencil also is used to retrace the pattern lines for transferring. Paint the designs with **acrylic craft paints**, which are available in a huge array of pre-mixed colors and come packaged in convenient plastic squeeze bottles. A **disposable plate** can be used for a palette—place small amounts of each color in puddles on the plate. Use **round brushes** to apply color, **flat brushes** to blend colors, and a **liner brush** for painting details.

### Supplies for Design Painting:

1. *Disposable plate, used for a palette*
2. *Acrylic craft paint*
3. *Artist's liner brush, for fine line work*
4. *Artist's flat brush*
5. *Artist's round brush*
6. *Design traced on tracing paper, ready for transfer to surface*
7. *Pencil*

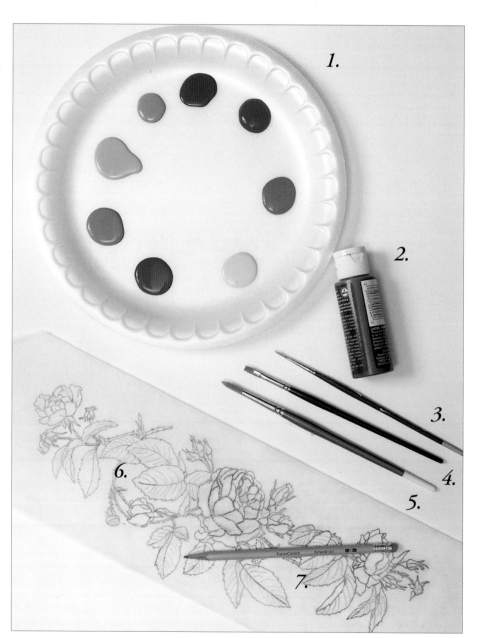

## DESIGN PAINTING TIPS

- Use round brushes to apply color.
- Lightly pounce with the tips of a small flat brush to blend colors.
- Use a liner brush for painting details.
- Paint the design in the order given in the project instructions.
- If, at any point, your traced pattern isn't visible, let the paint dry, reposition the pattern, and retrace the design.

# COUNTRYSIDE TULIPS BORDER

## *1*
## *Supplies*

**Acrylic Craft Paint:**

| | |
|---|---|
| Light green | Deep teal green |
| Yellow green | Red |
| Yellow | Pink |
| White | Medium blue |
| Pale blue | |

**Artist's Paint Brushes:**
Rounds - #5, #8
Flat - #12
Glaze - 3/4"

**Tools & Equipment:**
Sandpaper
Low tack masking tape
Disposable plates or palette
Tracing paper and pencil
Rag
Water container

## *2*
## *Transfer the Pattern*

1. Enlarge the pattern in this book on a copy machine.
2. Trace the pattern on one side of the tracing paper; then turn the paper over and trace the design on the other side.
3. Position the tracing on the wall and secure with masking tape. Trace over the design with a pencil (this will transfer the design to the wall). Reposition the tracing and repeat until the entire border is complete.

## *3*
## *Painting*

1. Squeeze small amounts of each paint color on a disposable plate. *Optional:* Add a drop of water to each color so the paint will flow smoothly on the surface.
2. Paint the tulips and leaves within the pattern lines, using photos as guides for color placement and strokes. Use one brush per color or rinse the brush in water and blot dry on a rag when changing colors. Do not use a wet brush—this will cause the paint to run. Allow to dry. ❧

## Design Pattern for Painting
*Enlarge pattern on copy machine to size needed for your design area.*

# ROSE GARLAND HIGHBOY

*This antique highboy was painted white, with soft green trim. A rose cluster embellishes one drawer, and a garland of rosebuds circles the top. Painted leaves adorn the drawer pulls, the lower drawer and apron, and the legs. After painting, the surface is antiqued for a mellow look. A matte sealer is a good choice for this aged, antique look.*

## 1
## Supplies

**Surface:** Wooden highboy

**Latex Paint:**
Soft green
White, flat or satin sheen

**Acrylic Craft Paint:**

| | |
|---|---|
| Poetry Green | Clover |
| Thicket | English Mustard |
| Spring Rose | Raspberry Sherbet |
| Raspberry Wine | Chocolate Fudge |

**Medium & Sealer:**
Brown antiquing medium
Matte acrylic sealer

**Artist's Paint Brushes:**
Rounds - #5, #6, #7, #8
Liner
Flat - #4

**Tools & Equipment:**
Sandpaper
Low tack masking tape
Disposable plates or palette
Small paint roller
Foam brush and/or bristle brush
2 cellulose sponges
Water container, Rag
Tracing paper and pencil
*Optional:* Electric sander
**Step-by-step photos on page 114.**

## 2
## Preparation

1. Remove drawer pulls. Sand the wood surface. Wipe away dust.
2. Brush or roll 2-3 coats of white paint on the surface. (Using a roller allows you to work faster, especially on a piece like this one that has a lot of flat areas.) Allow to dry completely.
3. Using photographs as guides, tape off the edges of the drawers and all the areas that will be painted green. Use photos as guides for color placement.

4. Paint masked off areas with soft green paint, using a 1" foam brush for larger areas and a #5 or #8 artist's round brush for small, tight areas. Allow to dry thoroughly. Remove tape.

## 3
## Transferring the Pattern

1. Enlarge the pattern in this book on a copy machine to an appropriate size for your furniture piece.
2. Trace the pattern on one side of the tracing paper; then turn the paper over and trace the design on the other side.
3. Position the design, right side up, on the surface and trace over the pattern lines **(photos 1 and 2 on page 114)**.

## 4
## Painting the Design

1. Squeeze about 1/2 teaspoon of each paint color on a disposable plate, keeping the colors separate. Mix 1-2 drops of water with each color.
2. Paint roses and rosebuds with spring rose and raspberry sherbet **(photo 3)**.
3. Shade petals with raspberry wine.
4. Paint leaves with poetry green or clover **(photo 4)**. Shade with thicket. Varying the colors makes the leaves look more natural. Each leaf picks up its own tone, depending on the way the colors are blended and how much of the base color shows through the shading. Allow to dry.
5. Paint veins, using the pointed tip of the round brush to pull the lines **(photo 4)**.
6. Add highlights with English mustard to leaves and petals.
7. Paint stems with green colors. Paint woody, thorny stems with Chocolate Fudge.

## 5
## Antiquing and Finishing

1. Remove any stray pencil marks from the white surface by rubbing with a soft, damp cloth. Allow to dry.
2. Seal the surface with matte sealer to protect. Allow to dry 24 hours.
3. Moisten both cellulose sponges. Squeeze out excess water. Use one sponge to stroke antiquing medium on the surface. Use the other sponge to lighten any areas that seem too harsh or too dark. Allow to dry thoroughly—24 hours.
4. Seal the surface with 2-3 coats of matte sealer. ✄

*Palette*

Spring Rose   Raspberry Sherbet   Raspberry Wine   Chocolate Fudge

Poetry Green   Clover   Thicket   English Mustard

# ROSE GARLAND HIGHBOY

## HERE'S HOW

**1**

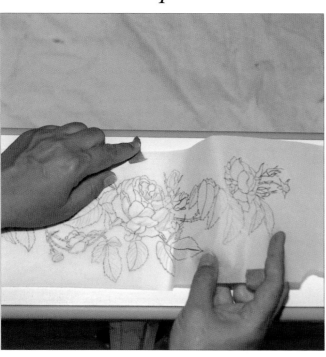

**2**

**3**

**4**

## Design Patterns for Painting

*Enlarge on copy machine to size needed for your funiture piece.*
*Refer to photo for pattern placement.*

# FLOWER GARDEN CHEST

*Charming, colorful flowers and plaid borders decorate the larger drawers of this painted chest. A painted dresser scarf extends playfully over the front edge, and the same plaid embellishes pulls on the smaller drawers.*

## 1
## Supplies

**Latex Paint:** White, flat or satin sheen

**Acrylic Craft Paint:**
Deep spruce green
Spruce green
Buttercup
Harvest gold
Cherry royale
Spring rose
Purple lilac
Royal purple

**Artist's Paint Brushes:**
Rounds - #5, #8
Flat #12
Liner

**Tools & Equipment:**
Tracing paper and pencil
Low tack masking tape
Sandpaper, 220 grit
Small paint roller
Bristle or foam brushes

## 2
## Preparation

1. Remove drawer pulls. Sand surface of chest. Wipe away dust.
2. Basecoat chest and pulls with white paint, using enough coats to achieve solid coverage. Let dry between coats. Let final coat dry thoroughly.

## 3
## Transferring the Pattern

1. Enlarge the patterns in this book (page 118) on a copy machine to an appropriate size for your furniture piece. There's one pattern for each flower design (four in all) and a pattern for the front edge of the dresser scarf.
2. Trace the patterns on one side of the tracing paper; then turn the paper over and trace the design on the other side.
3. Position the patterns, right side up, on the surface. Secure with tape. Trace over the pattern lines. Turn each of the flower patterns so the designs on facing drawers are mirror images.

## 4
## Painting the Plaid

1. With masking tape, mask off a border about 1-1/2" wide on the edges of the larger drawers.
2. To create the plaid, paint intersecting horizontal and vertical lines of deep spruce green and spruce green. See photo for placement.
3. Paint the plaid on the pulls for the smaller drawers.
4. Paint the same plaid on the front edge of the dresser scarf. There appears to be a darker scarf under the plaid one. Paint it with deep spruce green; then add a plaid of spruce green.
5. Continue to paint the plaid on the top of the chest, using photo as a guide for placement. (The lines don't have to be straight; these are wiggly, like a slightly rumpled piece of cloth.)

## 3
## Painting the Flowers

*See the instructions and photos for the Rose Painted Highboy for details of painting technique.*

1. Squeeze about 1/2 teaspoon of each paint color on a disposable plate, keeping the colors separate. Mix 1-2 drops of water with each color.
2. Paint tulips with spring rose and cherry royale.
3. Paint magnolia blossoms with buttercup and harvest gold. Accent with cherry royale.
4. Paint roses with spring rose and cherry royale.
5. Paint lilacs with purple lilac and royal purple.
6. Paint leaves with spruce green. Shade with deep spruce green. Allow to dry.

## 4
## Finishing

1. Remove any stray pencil marks from the white surface by rubbing with a soft, damp cloth. Allow to dry.
2. Seal the surface with 2-3 coats of matte sealer. 🐝

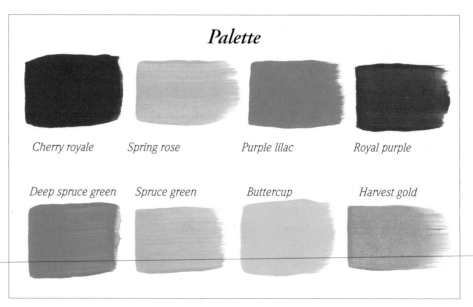

*Palette*

Cherry royale    Spring rose    Purple lilac    Royal purple

Deep spruce green    Spruce green    Buttercup    Harvest gold

# FLOWER GARDEN CHEST

## Design Pattern for Painting
*Enlarge on copy machine to size needed for your furniture piece.*

# CATCH OF THE DAY ARMOIRE

*This armoire was given a pickled finish and painted with tromphe l'oeil designs of fish, hooks, and flies that are meant to look as though pages from an old book were tacked on the door panels and sides.*

## 1
## Supplies

**Surface:** Wooden armoire

**Latex Wall Paint:**
White
Off-white
Glazing medium

**Acrylic Craft Paint:**
Black
Charcoal gray
Barn wood
Honeycomb
English mustard
Nutmeg
Chocolate fudge
Warm white
School bus yellow
Pure orange
Brick red
Pink
Thicket
Green meadow
Grass green

Fresh foliage
Azure blue
Light periwinkle
French blue
Teal
Dove gray

**Medium & Sealers:**
Blending medium
Matte acrylic sealer spray
Waterbase varnish, matte finish

**Artist's paint brushes:**
Round - #8
Liner brush
Flat - #12

**Tools & Equipment:**
Craft knife
Tracing paper and pencil
Foam brush and/or 3" paint roller
Sea sponge
Fine tip permanent marker
Steel wool, fine
Masking tape

## 2
## Preparation

1. Sand the wood surface. Wipe away dust.
2. Make a stain by mixing 3 parts glazing medium and 1 part white paint. Brush or wipe on the stain with a sponge. Let more of the white glaze settle in crevices and corners. Allow to dry.
3. Seal with one light coat of matte sealer. Allow to dry.
4. Lightly buff the surface with steel wool to etch the surface and prepare it for decorative painting.

## 3
## Transfer the Pattern and Paint the Pages

*Note: Patterns are found on pages 124 - 125.*
1. Enlarge the designs to the size you want, using a copy machine.
2. Trace the designs on tracing paper,

*Continued on page 122*

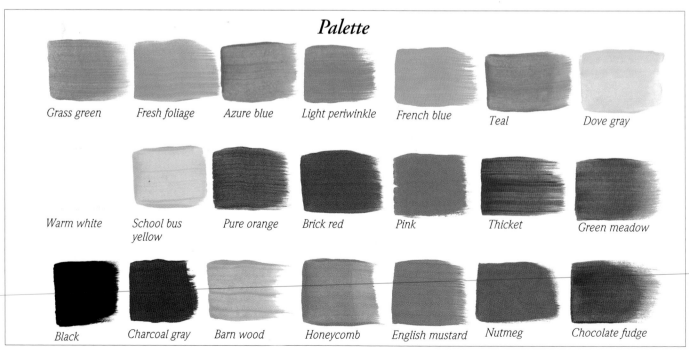

*Palette*

Grass green    Fresh foliage    Azure blue    Light periwinkle    French blue    Teal    Dove gray

Warm white    School bus yellow    Pure orange    Brick red    Pink    Thicket    Green meadow

Black    Charcoal gray    Barn wood    Honeycomb    English mustard    Nutmeg    Chocolate fudge

# CATCH OF THE DAY ARMOIRE

*Continued from page 120*

including outlines of the pages; then turn the paper over and trace the designs on the other side.

3. Position the traced designs on the armoire to determine placement for the designs. Place masking tape in the areas where the outlines of the pages will be **(photo 1)**. (You will make a tape stencil for the page outlines.) Press the tape firmly against the surface.

4. Position the pattern over the tape and trace the page outlines.

5. With a craft knife, lightly score the tape on the traced outlines. Don't press too hard; you want to cut only the tape, not the wood. Remove the tape inside the outlines. (This will be the shape of the pages.)

6. Using a roller or a foam brush, apply 1-2 coats off-white paint, making sure the wood is completely covered. Allow to dry. Leave the tape in place **(photo 2)**.

7. Mix 2 teaspoons of English mustard paint with a half cup of glazing medium. Moisten sponge and squeeze out excess water. Lightly pat off-white areas with the glaze mixture to create the yellowed, worn look of old parchment paper.

8. Add 1 small drop of chocolate fudge paint to the glaze mixture. Sponge the areas again, concentrating the darker color on some edges, making them a little darker, so it looks as if the paper has aged more in some areas than in others. Allow to dry.

9. Transfer the details (the fish, the lettering, nails and pins, and the turned edges of the paper).

10. With the remaining glaze mixture, shade the turned corners and edges of the pages, using a #5 or #8 round brush.

## 4
## *Painting the Design*

1. Paint the pins and tacks that appear to be holding the paper and the stringer with black.

2. Remove the masking tape.

3. On a disposable plate, squeeze out a small amount of each paint color and mix each color with blending medium, using 3 parts paint and 1 part medium.

4. Paint the fish, one at a time, using photos as guides for color placement. Apply layers of color so some areas are deeply shaded and others are very pale **(photo 3)**. Using a #12 flat brush, stipple the fish to remove visible brush strokes and soften and blend colors slightly.

5. Use a liner brush to paint details (eyes, mouths, gills, dots, scales) with chocolate fudge.

## 5
## *Finishing*

1. Use a fine tip permanent marker for the lettering **(photo 4)**. Allow to dry.

2. Mist the painted areas with matte sealer spray to protect and prevent bleeding. Allow to dry.

3. Seal the armoire with 2-3 coats liquid matte sealer. Allow to dry between coats. For a smooth, professional finish, buff the surface in between coats with steel wool and wipe away dust before applying the next coat. 🍂

*Photo 1*

*Photo 2*

*Photo 3*

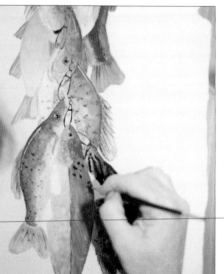

*Photo 4*

Caudal fin

Hand Tied Flies

orn Fly

Quill
Dry Fly

Winged
Wet Fly

KIRBY-6
KIRBY-16
CARLISLE - 1
CARLISLE - 2

LIMERICK-3/0

# CATCH OF THE DAY ARMOIRE

## Design Patterns for Painting

*Enlarge patterns on copy machine to size needed for your furniture piece.*

# • Catch of the Day Armoire •

*Refer to photo for placement of patterns*

*Patterns continue on page 126*

# CATCH OF THE DAY ARMOIRE

## Design Patterns for Painting

*Enlarge on copy machine to size needed for your furniture piece.*
*Refer to photo for placement of patterns.*

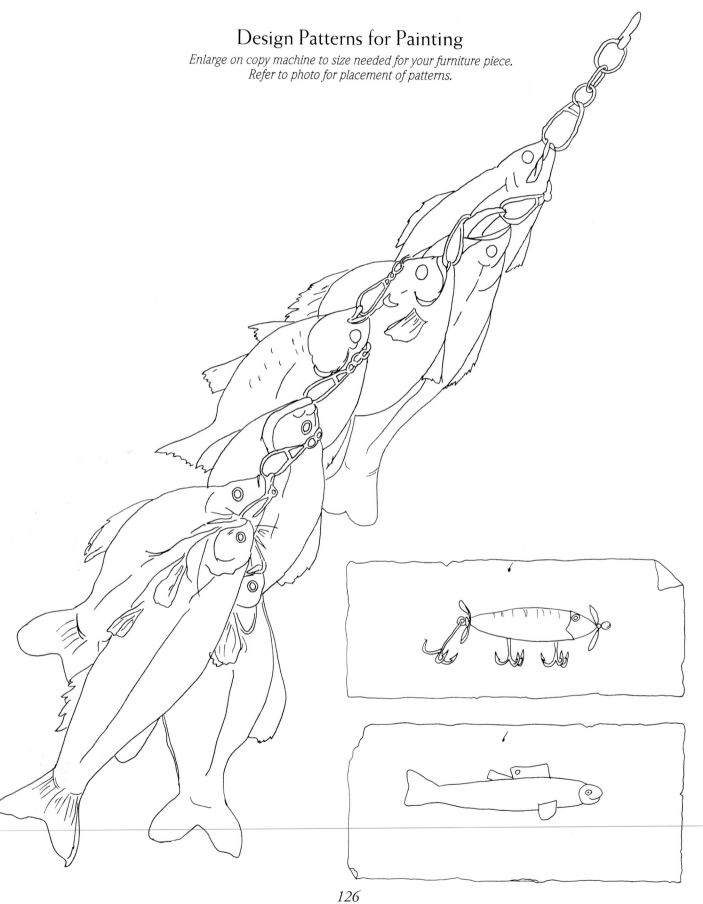

126

# Metric Conversions

## Inches to Millimeters and Centimeters

| Inches | MM | CM |
|--------|-----|------|
| 1/8 | 3 | .3 |
| 1/4 | 6 | .6 |
| 3/8 | 10 | 1.0 |
| 1/2 | 13 | 1.3 |
| 5/8 | 16 | 1.6 |
| 3/4 | 19 | 1.9 |
| 7/8 | 22 | 2.2 |
| 1 | 25 | 2.5 |
| 1-1/4 | 32 | 3.2 |
| 1-1/2 | 38 | 3.8 |
| 1-3/4 | 44 | 4.4 |
| 2 | 51 | 5.1 |
| 2-1/2 | 64 | 6.4 |
| 3 | 76 | 7.6 |
| 3-1/2 | 89 | 8.9 |
| 4 | 102 | 10.2 |
| 5 | 127 | 12.7 |
| 6 | 152 | 15.2 |
| 7 | 178 | 17.8 |
| 8 | 203 | 20.3 |
| 9 | 229 | 22.9 |
| 10 | 254 | 25.4 |
| 11 | 279 | 27.9 |
| 12 | 305 | 30.5 |

## Yards to Meters

| Yards | Meters |
|-------|--------|
| 1/8 | .11 |
| 1/4 | .23 |
| 3/8 | .34 |
| 1/2 | .46 |
| 5/8 | .57 |
| 3/4 | .69 |
| 7/8 | .80 |
| 1 | .91 |
| 1-1/2 | 1.37 |
| 1-5/8 | 1.49 |
| 1-3/4 | 1.60 |
| 1-7/8 | 1.71 |
| 2 | 1.83 |
| 2-1/2 | 2.29 |
| 3 | 2.74 |
| 4 | 3.66 |
| 5 | 4.57 |
| 6 | 5.49 |
| 7 | 6.40 |
| 8 | 7.32 |
| 9 | 8.23 |
| 10 | 9.14 |

*Marbleized Wainscotting Panes:* See instructions on page 30.

# INDEX